"HE HANDLES A BASKETBALL THE WAY THE AVERAGE PERSON HANDLES A TENNIS BALL. HE CAN RAISE ONE ARM ABOVE ANOTHER PLAYER'S TWO OUTSTRETCHED HANDS AND SNATCH THE BALL AS THOUGH HE'S TAKING A HANDFUL OF POPCORN. OR HE CAN BE RUNNING AT FULL SPEED, REACH DOWN TO THE FLOOR, PICK UP A ROLLING BALL OR A BOUNCE PASS WITH ONE HAND AND SHOOT THE BALL WITHOUT USING THE OTHER. OR HE CAN BE STANDING WITH HIS DEFENSIVE MAN LEANING ON HIM, CALL FOR A PASS FROM A TEAMMATE, REACH OUT ONE HAND AND CATCH THE PASS LIKE A FIRST BASE-MAN CATCHING A THROW. . . . THERE ARE THINGS HE CAN DO THAT NO ONE ELSE HAS EVER DONE . . . REASONS WHY EVERYONE WHO HAS SEEN HIM COMES AWAY TELLING STORIES ABOUT DR. J."

—from *The Legend of Dr. J.*

"One of the better sports biographies, and obviously a labor of love, about the closest thing to a superman playing basketball today."   —*Lewiston Journal*

ABOUT THE AUTHOR

Marty Bell has been watching Julius Erving play basketball since they were both in high school on Long Island. Bell was formerly a senior editor at *Sport Magazine* and *New Times* magazine. His other books include *Carnival at Forest Hills* and two novels, *Breaking Balls* and *No Hard Feelings*.

The Legend of Dr. J

MARTY BELL

Newly Updated and Expanded

A SIGNET BOOK

SIGNET
Published by the Penguin Group
Penguin Books USA Inc., 375 Hudson Street,
New York, New York 10014, U.S.A.
Penguin Books Ltd, 27 Wrights Lane,
London W8 5TZ, England
Penguin Books Australia Ltd, Ringwood,
Victoria, Australia
Penguin Books Canada Ltd, 2801 John Street,
Markham, Ontario, Canada L3R 1B4
Penguin Books (N.Z.) Ltd, 182–190 Wairau Road,
Auckland 10, New Zealand

Penguin Books Ltd, Registered Offices:
Harmondsworth, Middlesex, England

Published by arrangement with Coward McCann & Geoghegan, Inc.

First Signet Printing, February, 1976
18   17   16   15   14   13   12   11   10

Copyright © 1975, 1981 by Marty Bell
Copyright © 1976, 1977 by New American Library, a division of
Penguin Books USA Inc.
Cover photograph: Copyright © 1981 Royden Hobson/Focus on Sports

 REGISTERED TRADEMARK—MARCA REGISTRADA

Printed in the United States of America

For Florence and Jerry Bell

Acknowledgments

My greatest pleasure while investigating the life of Julius Erving came from meeting the people who have played a role in that life. For their kind and candid cooperation I want to thank Don Ryan, Earl Moseley, Ray Wilson, Kevin Loughery, Rod Thorn, Barney Kremenko, Roy Boe, Bob Carlson, Brian Taylor, George Carter, Bill Putnam, Mike Storen, Mike Recht, Jack Leaman, Al Bianchi and especially Dave Brownbill. I am envious of the nice collection of people who have always surrounded Julius. I also want to thank three devoted fans, one named Julius and two others who asked me to change their names for this book.

Matt Merola and Paul Getz came to me with this project in the first place, Dick Schaap was kind enough to allow me the time to complete it, and Peggy Brooks was always there to guide me through it. I am indebted to each of them. And a special thanks to Harriet Bell, who as always was patient and understanding throughout.

I am often told that writing a book is a very lonely experience. But all these people made it a lot less lonely and always enjoyable.

Contents

1. Me and Julius
Down by the Schoolyard

I discovered Julius Erving quite by accident.

It was early winter in 1967. I was a senior in high school on Long Island. It was more than a year before Martin Luther King and Bobby Kennedy would be gunned down and everyone would be scared into becoming political. Meanwhile, we all still wore penny loafers, cuffed pants, and short hair. We drank beer in cars parked behind deserted supermarkets, because we weren't old enough to drink it anyplace else. And we looked forward to sporting events as our biggest social activities.

At Mepham High School in Bellmore, New York, wrestling was the most popular sport. It was as closely associated with the school as gambling is with Las Vegas. It was more than twenty five years since Mepham had won ninety-nine straight matches, lost one, and then won one hundred more. But we still felt the effects of that streak. Anyone with any thoughts of being a school hero wrestled. Even Lenny Bruce (then Schneider) wrestled when he went there.

There were only a handful of blacks in the neighborhood. And all the good Catholic basketball players were recruited by the parochial high schools. Our school was left with the Catholic kids who lacked either the talent or the intelligence to get recruited, and all of us little Jewish kids. At five-feet-eight, I could see over most of the heads in the hallway between classes. So I guess we

1

embraced wrestling out of necessity. Basketball was something we went elsewhere to see.

My friend Mark Falkowitz had a girlfriend who was a cheerleader for South Side High School in Rockville Centre. Mark explained that their school had eight black males taller than five-feet-ten and so they were assured of a good basketball team.

One Tuesday afternoon in November he told me that South Side would be playing at Roosevelt High School, a predominantly black school located just two towns west of Bellmore. He suggested that since we were "frustrated basketball buffs in a mecca for wrestling," we ought to take advantage of the opportunity and go see the two black teams play ball.

What he was really suggesting was that since I was his only friend who had a driver's license, I should drive him to see his girlfriend Eileen cheer.

A good basketball game was always a treat. And I thought Eileen might have some nice-looking friends among the cheerleaders. So I agreed to go.

We both came away from that game raving.

Mark raved about Eileen's thighs, which were prominently displayed beneath the red and yellow of her uniform.

I raved about the most exciting basketball player I had ever seen on the Island. He was a six-foot-two junior named Julius Erving.

Erving didn't start that game for Roosevelt. Five burly seniors did. They would stampede up the court and one of them would throw up a gangly shot that would carom off the wooden backboards. The other four would knock aside the South Side players like duckpins and congregate under the basket, waiting to rebound the ball and lay it up for an easy basket. They had all the grace of Alex Karras. They scared their opponents into losing.

But midway through the first quarter the Roosevelt coach took out one of his bulls and inserted the spindly legged Erving. Suddenly the whole rhythm of the game changed. The four remaining bulls were more leisurely in their approach. And more respectful of their bruised opponents' well-being.

Now Roosevelt came on the court and simply gave the ball to Erving. His body the color of regular coffee, his hair cropped close to his head, his wide, innocent eyes filled with excitement, he was a young boy with the body control of an accomplished ballet dancer. He put the ball to the floor once and then again and weaved and twisted his way between the other nine players. He glided gracefully up into the air, above all the others and dropped the ball in the basket with ease. He was a thing of beauty and all eyes were magnetically drawn to him. All except Falkowitz's.

Mark's enthusiasm for Eileen wouldn't last much beyond that afternoon. But my enthusiasm for Julius Erving would become my favorite topic of conversation whenever I talked sports.

The American audience likes to possess performers. We discover them at the first blossoming of their careers, before anyone else we know has seen them. From then on following them becomes one of our hobbies. We begin to talk of them in the same possessive tones in which we speak about our children and our lovers. If they are a Joe Namath or a Barbra Streisand, we get pleasure from following their ascent. If they fade quickly, our pleasure comes from reminiscing about what might have been.

Following Erving became one of my hobbies. When I was at the library to study during my freshman year of college (his senior year of high school), I would stop in the periodical room and peek into *Newsday*, the Long Island newspaper, to see what he was up to. When he left Roosevelt and went to the University of Massachusetts, he became somewhat easier to follow, although

not as easy as if he were at a more accomplished basketball school.

I saw him play in college, and I saw him more often
when he left college after his junior year to accept a
half-million dollars from the Virginia Squires of the
American Basketball Association. By then he had grown
to six-feet-six and had filled out to a solid two hundred
pounds underneath a full Afro. He compiled impressive
statistics at Massachusetts and averaged 27 points and 15
rebounds per game in his first year in the pros. But I
didn't realize the widespread effects of his talents until
I saw him play in the Rucker League in Harlem after his
first pro season.

I arrived at the Holcombe Rucker Playground at 155th
Street and Eighth Avenue at 1:30 on a July Saturday
afternoon. It was still two hours until the game was
scheduled to begin, but there wasn't an empty spot to
squeeze into around the fenced-in asphalt court. Kids
who had gotten there too late to find a seat in the
crowded bleachers hung from the wire fence and the
trees behind it. Some even climbed to the roof of the
adjacent school. Across the street eyes peered through
binoculars sticking out of the sixteenth-floor windows
of the apartment buildings that filled the space where
the Polo Grounds once stood. Hard-driving soul sounds
came from radios knowingly tuned to the same station
and the adults and children forced to stand behind the
baskets because of the size of the crowd passed the time
by rhythmically swaying back and forth. The strong,
pungent smell of marijuana pierced the humid air.

At around three o'clock the players began to arrive.
The whole scene was turned on by then, like a Saturday
night in a dark basement club rather than an afternoon
on the playground. Then Julius Erving made his
appearance.

The Doctor. Doctor J., the crowd murmured.

Watch him operate on the court.

It was here a year before that this young rebel, who had announced that he was leaving college to sign a pro basketball contract, had coined his own nickname.

Nicknames are common in all sports, but in no place are they as widepread as in basketball. Doug Smith, one of too few black writers covering sports, explained to me that most black children are given nicknames within their families when they are growing up. It gives them something all their own to be proud of. It makes them special. Basketball, having more black players than any other sport, takes on the most aspects of black culture, including nicknames.

The story goes that the first time Julius Erving showed up at the Rucker Playground, the public-address announcer found himself searching for ways to describe the previously unheard-of performer. He began affixing all of the most banal nicknames on Julius. The Claw. Black Moses. Magic. Little Hawk.

But during one of the time-outs, Julius walked over to him and said, "Just call me the Doctor."

He did. It stuck.

As he joined the line of players prepared to begin the lay-up drill, you could feel everyone in the stands lean in a little closer. They knew what to anticipate.

Each player took his turn rising above the rim and dunking the ball down, hard, through the metal chain net. The people in the crowd held their breaths, anticipating each dunk, and then exploded into a harmonious cheer. Basketball is the only major spectator sport that limits the opportunities for a player to display violent anger. In baseball you smack the ball or slide hard. In football or hockey you lunge into your opponent. In the smooth flow of a basketball game, the dunk is the emotional release—for the shooter and for the crowd.

Erving reached the front of the lay-up line. He took the ball easily into his oversized hands and casually bounced it twice on the blacktop. He left the ground

behind the foul line and soared toward the basket. He braced himself on the rim with one hand and threw the ball down through the hoop with the other. The ball bounced on the asphalt, came up ten feet into the air and went through the hoop again.

The place went into a frenzy. Everyone ceremoniously slapped hands. The fence and trees began to shake. Confetti came down from the sixteenth floor. If the scene had been indoors, the roof would have had to struggle to remain aloft.

But that was only the beginning. The game began. The five players from each team ran up and down the court in no set patterns, trying to put the ball in the basket more times than the opposition. Each one looked for every opportunity to shoot. Passing was something they did only when they did not have a shot. They worked for their shots by *putting on a move.*

The *move* is the most basic element of the schoolyard basketball. It occurs when one basketball player has the ball and is being closely guarded by another. The player with the ball puts it to the floor, begins to dribble, and bobs and weaves his way up and down or side to side until he has eluded the man who is guarding him and has cleared himself for a shot at the basket.

In a team game, when success is based on the co-ordination of the five players, the move is not so important. But in the playgrounds, where it is one player against one, the move is everything. For the players who grew up in the playground, it is a means of expression. When a player *puts a move* on his opponent and scores a basket, he is embarrassing his opponent. He is asserting his strength. The only way his opponent can regain his own respect is by creating an equally unique move.

There is really no means of personal expression like the move in any other sport. It is rather like the performance of an uninhibited ballet dancer. An Isadora

Duncan. And so basketball people come to the parks and the schoolyards to see moves and hope to come away with stories about them.

Basketball folklore has it that the best moves were created by Connie Hawkins in this same Rucker Playground and by Elgin Baylor who played his schoolyard ball in Washington, D.C. But from the first days on the playground in Roosevelt Julius was altering that folklore. He was clearly the best playground player anyone had ever seen.

Without the patterned offense of college or the pros to limit him, Julius ran up and down the court that day free-lancing his way to 53 points. There was no scoreboard and no one in the crowd knew the score. No one cared. When it was apparently over, an official announced that the score was tied, and that there would be an overtime. The crowd loved it. "You can't get enough of Dr. J.," shouted a ten-year-old in a floppy yellow hat behind me. I agreed.

Sitting there among a crowd to whom basketball was sacred, I realized that my own initial reaction to Erving was not unique.

Each of the 3,000 or so people there felt the same personal attachment to him. They would all leave the scene with new Julius Erving stories for their own well-used repertoires. They would all tell those stories in the familiar possessive tones. They were all helping to create the legend of Dr. J.

The game of basketball encourages the evolution of such folklore. Professional baseball or football or hockey requires the organization the sports leagues have provided. You need too many people, too much organization to play an impromptu pickup game. But a high-quality basketball game is the simplest of all the games to put together. And some of the best basketball is played in the schoolyards, away from the coaches, away from the statisticians, away from the press. These games are recorded nowhere but in the memories of the people who are fortunate enough to have come out to watch. And they are described to the rest of the fans in their words. Often, by the time we hear them, they are exaggerated.

Charlie Rosen, a former basketball player in the Eastern League and now a teacher of Chaucer at a small New York college, likes to tell about the time Kareem Abdul-Jabbar was playing against a local star in the Rucker Playground. The star ran around the seven-foot-four pro a few times. Finally Kareem went up in the air and blocked one of his shots so hard that it flew over the fence and out onto Lenox Avenue. Just then a bus came up the street and ran over the ball.

And Pete Vecsey, a writer for the *Daily News* and coach of the team Julius plays on in the Rucker Tournament, likes to tell about the time Julius was trapped on the right side of the basket unable to shoot. He claims Julius jumped and threw the ball up against the backboard. While he was still in the air, he glided under the hoop, took his own rebound and stuffed it down through the hoop with two hands over his head.

I'm not really sure I believe either story. And yet who's going to believe my tale about Julius dunking the ball so hard it bounced up ten feet and went through the basket again?

This is how basketball legends begin. On asphalt courts. In hot cities. In front of groups of people who would rather be there, watching a game, than anyplace else in the world. In front of kids who wear their Converse sneakers to school every day and who use a hookshot motion whenever they throw something in the garbage can. In front of people whose frame of reference for everything in life is basketball.

"You should join my Y team, man," one devotee once said to his friend while they were shooting around together. "We get to see the world."

"Yeah? What you seen?" his friend asked.

"We been to Washington and New Orleans. And last year we even went to Switzerland."

"Switzerland? Man, how was Switzerland?"

"Bad," the boy answered. "We lost."

But the legends do not stay among these people, within their communities, for very long. The player of their affections becomes a professional. He becomes a commercial property. And just as I realized that everyone in that playground had the same possessive feelings about Julius that I had, they eventually must realize that they now share their prized possession with the bulk of New York's basketball fans.

But as exciting as Julius is, the legend of Dr. J. did not change from a neighborhood story to a metropolitan story because of anything he did with a basketball. In fact, many devotees of the legend have never seen him play. Instead they read about him—about how many points he scored. But more significantly about how much money he makes. In the great tradition of show biz Julius Erving became a New York star overnight. And he didn't even have to put on his uniform to do it.

2. The Caper

On the afternoon of July 31, 1973, Roy Boe, a short-haired, gangly man in his early forties, sat at a desk in the Park Avenue law offices of the firm of Roth, Carlson and Spengler. In front of him were two checks made out for the amounts of $425,000 and $750,000. He signed them both. He then signed a contract that would cost him $2,800,000 over a period of eight years.

The check for the lesser amount was for John Wilcox, the president of the Omni Corporation in Atlanta, which owned a basketball team named the Hawks. The check for the larger amount was for Earl Foreman, a Washington-based lawyer who owned a team called the Virginia Squires.

The contract was passed to Irwin Weiner, a red-headed man of medium height, dressed in a flashy suit and exhibiting a noticeably large gold and diamond ring when he reached for the long cigar in his mouth. Weiner is an agent who represents athletes. Next to Weiner was a tall, thin black man with a stubble of hair showing on his chin. He signed the name Julius Erving to the contract. All the men stood and shook hands with each other.

Just four years earlier Boe had paid $988,000 to a man named Arthur Brown to purchase a franchise in the American Basketball Association named the New York Nets. Now he was pledging $4,000,000 to obtain the services of one player. That was probably more money than the Nets had grossed in the four years he had been their owner. It was thought to be the most expensive deal involving just one player in sports history. It had taken seven lawyers more than two weeks to work it out.

"It was like closing on a house," Boe said.

"It was more like a closing on a bank," said Weiner.

Boe, who had made his fortune in dresses, was now spending it to get rid of suits. In 1971 Erving had signed a contract with the Virginia Squires of the American Basketball Association for $500,000 over four years.

In 1972 Erving had signed a contract with the Atlanta Hawks of the National Basketball Association for $2,-000,000 over five years. At the same time his agent, Weiner, had filed suit against the Squires to rescind that contract, claiming they had violated their obligation.

Erving was prepared to leave the ABA and join the NBA. But there was as much fighting over him within that league as there was between the two leagues. According to the rules governing the NBA, the Hawks had no claim to Erving's services. He was instead the property of the Milwaukee Bucks, who had chosen him in the annual college draft, the accepted procedure for acquiring talent. When Erving signed with the Hawks and appeared in two exhibition games in their uniform, Walter Kennedy, the commissioner of the NBA, fined the team $25,000 for ignoring the league's procedure. In response the Hawks and Erving filed suit against the league for $2,000,000 claiming the draft was a violation of the Sherman Antitrust Act.

The Bucks, meanwhile, sat back, taking it for granted that the problem would be settled in the league's favor, avoiding committing any of their own money to legal fees.

What Boe had done on this hot summer day was to pay off the two teams who had contracts with Erving and suits in court. They, in turn, agreed to destroy those contracts and to drop the legal action they had been pursuing. The Hawks, a struggling franchise with a high payroll, were happy to free themselves of the controversy and to take the money. The Squires, who were reported to be close to bankruptcy, accepted the money as operating capital along with a much lower priced player named George Carter and the draft rights to Kermit Washington, a senior at American University, whom they would never sign.

The Nets received Erving and were also forced to accept a player named Willie Sojourner, a high-priced substitute center who was said to be Erving's closest friend on the Squires.

Meanwhile, in Milwaukee, Wisconsin, the Bucks, who had spent nothing and signed nothing, received nothing. They had followed the rules to acquire Erving just as they had to acquire every other player who had ever performed for the team. But in this situation that was not good enough. They did not have a contract with Erving's signature on it, and so they were left with no legal complaints.

"This is the rottenest caper I have ever seen," said William Alverson, the Bucks' president.

*　　*　　*

The Nets called a press conference for noon the next day. It was held at the Dover House, a Long Island restaurant owned by composer Burt Bacharach, and located just a few miles from the Nassau Coliseum, where the Nets played their home games.

There Boe confirmed what Earl Foreman had leaked to the press immediately after the signing the day before. Julius Erving, who five years earlier had left his home in Roosevelt to attend the University of Massachusetts and then went to Virginia to play for the Virginia Squires, was coming home to Long Island to play for the Nets.

"We're in a business," Boe announced, "and in a business you have to do things this way. You do things the way you build a factory.

"This is an important move for our franchise, but not a critical one. I know that one player will not draw consistently. In basketball you have to win to draw. You have to win during the season and you have to win in the playoffs. The playoffs are the difference between making money and losing money to every team in basketball except the Knicks and the Lakers.

"I'm making an investment, figuring with Julius Erving on our side, we're going to win."

The day was filled with excitement. Having watched Julius since high school, I felt a certain closeness to it all. I felt I was a part of all that was happening. I guess that's the feeling everyone involved in the production of sports wants the fan to have. And it was probably a feeling shared by all the local writers there that day.

And yet there were ironies that were being covered up by all the excitement. Certain facts were being brushed over by the glamor of Roy Roe's spending $4,000,000.

The reporters gathered around Boe and asked him for his own reasons for making the expenditure. The two things that he most mentioned were Julius' possibilities as a draw and as a winner. To date Julius had never really been either. As good an athlete as Julius was, Boe, according to his own terms, was investing in an unproven commodity.

On that day, Julius was probably the least-known superathlete in America. He had not played big-time college basketball and he had played pro ball in a floundering league with a majority of its teams in obscure cities. Athletes in cities as large as Chicago claimed they did not get enough national recognition. An athlete as great as Hank Aaron had to approach the most prestigious record in baseball before he got the attention he deserved because his career was based in Milwaukee and

Atlanta. So it followed that Julius was a nobody no matter how good he may have been in Norfolk, Virginia.

You could talk to sports fans around the country and you'd realize that only the most avid basketball fans even knew who Julius Erving was. For the ordinary player that might be fine, but to justify this kind of investment Boe's protégé had to become a household word. Like Namath or Aaron.

On the seven occasions that Julius had led the Squires into the Coliseum against the Nets in 1973 they had averaged 1,700 more fans than the 6,600 they averaged for the whole season. Even as Boe presented his new star to the New York press for the first time, almost a hundred people were lined up at the Coliseum ticket window ordering $350 season tickets. But these figures were not convincing enough. This was a local reaction to a hometown boy. Julius had to be more than that. He would have to become a metropolitan hero in New York. He would have to focus the public's attention on the Nets as Joe Namath had for the Jets and Tom Seaver had for the Mets. He was quickly awarded the same nickname that those other two highly paid stars had worn—*the franchise*. But Boe was investing ten times the original highly publicized investment in Namath. And he expected more for it. To him and his fellow owners Julius' nickname should have been *the league*.

As it happened, Julius Erving got more national recognition for signing this contract than he ever had for anything he did on the basketball court. Although it seems unlikely, it is possible that Boe paid less money to Atlanta and Virginia than was reported and maybe even less to Julius. But the $4,000,000 figure was a great publicity gimmick. New York and its press are fascinated by other people's money. When Michael Burke, then the president of the Yankees, wanted to pay his best player, Bobby Murcer, $100,000, he justified it to his board as a great public-relations move. And *New York* magazine has a strong-selling issue each year when they list salaries of noted New Yorkers right on the cover. Salaries are big news. And this contract was a big story.

Julius had never really been a winner either. His teams had always done well, but not well enough. The Squires had had their best season ever and finished in first place the year before Julius arrived. Each year he was there the team's record dropped off. He, of course, was not to blame. But still he had not won. Namath and Seaver had both made their bosses look like wise investors by leading their teams to championships. Boe expected Julius to do the same thing for him.

So this was the situation as Julius stood up to address the press in his money-green plaid sport jacket and bow tie. The whole day had turned into an event, just as the Nets wanted it to be. A well-financed event. Full of a lot of promises. Full of a lot of questions. The money had added dimension to the legend of Dr. J. And it would spread it further than it had ever been spread before. But now the Doctor had to go out and live up to the expanding legend. The $4,000,000 legend. Could any twenty-three-year-old kid justify such a wager? Especially one who had put himself in places where he avoided the nagging demands of national attention for his entire young life?

"I know that if I want to go down to the corner with a bottle and hang out, I can't," he said. "There are times when I have to let being Julius Erving keep me in check. But that's the price you pay for being a commodity."

"Doesn't all this put pressure on you?" someone asked.

"I put the most pressure on myself because of my ambitions to be the best basketball player ever. What happens around me can't put any more pressure on me than that."

3. Roots

The announcement was made. The caper completed. And most of the reporters walked out of the Dover House and to their cars to drive to their typewriters and make Julius famous.

One writer, Dave Anderson, the amiable sports columnist of the New York *Times*, asked Julius if he would drive with him to Roosevelt and visit the playground where he had spent much of his childhood.

Julius got into his white Avanti with his initials on the front license plate. He drove south on the Meadowbrook Parkway, past the Nassau Coliseum, the large, white, stone hatbox where he would be performing for the Nets. Within ten minutes he was on the tree-lined streets of Roosevelt, streets filled with small, boxlike houses, many with chipped paint and shingles and rubbed-out lawns.

Not too many years before, Julius had ridden his bicycle the mile from his house on Pleasant Avenue to Roosevelt Park. He would come out to play in shorts and a T-shirt and his Converse sneakers. Centennial Park was just up the block from his house, but the more talented kids hung out at Roosevelt. Julius was among the more talented kids.

This day he pulled up in his Avanti and got out, dressed in the green plaid sports jacket and velvet bow tie. And with a guarantee for almost three million dollars packed away in his pocket.

"When you were younger, how much money did you have in your pocket?" Anderson asked him.

"I always kept twenty-five or fifty cents with me," he said. "That was enough for a soda."

Roosevelt Park has tennis courts, handball courts, a playground for small children, and a lake surrounded by trees and grass. But the most well-trodden areas are the two green asphalt basketball courts neatly lined in white paint. In this community, where there isn't much spare money for other forms of entertainment, the park is the main attraction. It lures kids the way the Sirens lured Ulysses.

Julius walked out onto the court and slapped hands with some of the kids playing there. He had left there five years earlier to go to Massachusetts. He had stopped in Virginia and, for a short time, in Atlanta. But now he was home.

"My life-style has changed considerably," he said. "But I still want to identify with my roots. There are certain things you can't buy in life. I'm very much aware of that.

"There are things here I don't want to give up. Things like friendships and memories of people who have affected my growth and development."

He was born on February 22, 1950. George Washington's birthday.

Legend has it that a nurse walked into the hospital room and said to his mother, "Why don't you name him George Washington Erving since he was born today?"

"Have your own baby if you want to name him George Washington," his mother said. "I'm naming mine Julius Winfield Erving II."

Julius Winfield Erving I left home when Julius II was three years old. His wife, Callie Erving, raised her three children in a housing project on Linden Avenue in Hempstead. His sister, Alexis, was a few years older than Julius. His brother, Marvin, was a few years younger. His mother collected welfare and cleaned house—other people's.

Julius was a quiet, serious kid. "I was raised pretty much by one parent and she let me do what I wanted," he says. "I consciously tried to be aware of what was happening around me. If I was wrong, I was willing to take the consequences. I have to face up to the truth, be honest with myself.

"My sister was always extroverted and I was introverted. A lot of things happened where she thought I should react, but I didn't. She told me one day that I was going to explode, holding things in so much. She thought I was doing it on purpose. I remember in high school once somebody told me I acted like an old man."

There was a town park, Campbell Park, next to the project, and there Julius played his first basketball. When he was nine years old, he was five-feet-four and unusually graceful for a kid of his age. He had long arms, hands as big as any grown man's and strong, thick wrists. Andy Haggerty, the director of the park, felt Julius was the most talented young kid he had even seen playing ball there. So he introduced him to Don Ryan, who coached a team at the local Salvation Army Center for boys between the ages of ten and twelve. Ryan had grown up a block away from the center and played basketball at Hempstead High School. He was nineteen years old and a student at Adelphi University in Garden City when Julius was brought to him.

By the time he was eleven years old, Julius had grown to five-feet-six. But he already had great spring in his legs and combined with those big hands, he was able to out rebound kids who were more than six feet tall. There were two other good offensive ballplayers on the Salvation Army Center team, boys named Archie Rogers and Al Williams. Archie, Al, and Julius each averaged 11

points a game. But Julius was able to dominate a game
with his rebounding.

Ryan's team was easily the best on Long Island. They
won 27 and lost 3 when Julius was eleven, and won 31
and lost only 1 when Julius was twelve. So Ryan had
them sell candy door to door to raise money so they
could travel and play out-of-town teams. They could
afford to travel only as far as York, Pennsylvania, but it
was a new experience for kids who had until then gone
only as far as a bicycle would take them. Julius says that
Ryan always acted like one of the guys and made the
twelve-year-old kids feel much more grown up.

I went to visit Don Ryan at Hempstead High School,
where he teaches business and runs a student work program that places kids who need it in a spot where they
can make some money as part of their high school
education.

He is thirty-four years old now, still living with his
parents a block away from the Salvation Army Center
and still coaching the team there. His brown hair short
and parted and brushed to the right, his round, youthful
face highlighted by rosy cheeks, wearing a red alpaca
sweater whose style was once identified with Perry
Como, he must still look very much as he did when
Julius played for him fourteen years ago.

Ryan's whole life is dedicated to kids—those he
teaches and those he coaches. As we sat in his glass-
enclosed office in the ultramodern high school, some of
these kids kept knocking on his door. He would intro-
duce each one to me on the basis of his basketball accomplishments. And the kids would smile, embarrassed
by and proud of what their friend and coach was saying.
They all obviously played an important part in his life.
And in many cases he did the same for them.

"I always tried to be a friend to my players," he says.
"Since I lived so close to the center, I used to have them

over to meet my parents. The first time I had Julius over, he introduced himself to my mother and told her that he had won a poetry-reading contest at Prospect School in Hempstead. Then he recited a poem for her. My mother was so impressed. Even today, when she tells someone about Julius, she talks about that poem."

I asked Don if in Julius' case he felt he had to be a little more than a friend.

"You mean because he didn't have a father?" he asked. I nodded. "That's hard to say. I tried to spend time with him and show interest all the time. Julius liked to find a church wherever we went. I remember once when our team traveled to York, Pennsylvania, he asked me to go to church with him. We went to a place called the Shiloh Baptist Church, and it was the first black church I had ever gone to. The people just stood up and shouted whenever they felt like it. I had never seen anything like it.

"I also tried to get a little friendly with the rest of his family. He was real close with his brother Marvin, you know. One day I saw Marvin playing basketball in a park and I went over and said, 'How you doing?'

"He said, 'Not as good as Julius. But I'm president of my class in school.' You could tell he thought his brother was the greatest, but he wanted to have something of his own.

"So I said, 'Well, Julius will be a basketball star and you'll be the senator from New York.'

"You never know what effect you have on any kids. Julius went on to play basketball, but his teammate Archie Rogers is a three-time loser. Been in jail three times for assault and robbery. His parole officer just recently called me to get up $70,000. But I couldn't do that.

"Last year my team had this barbecue in one of the kids' backyards, and both Julius and Archie were there. It was the first time they had seen each other in a long time. I just kind of sat in the corner and stared at the two of them out of the corner of my eye. The two stars of my best team. One was a pro superstar. The other was a convict. You always wonder how responsible you were in getting both of them where they were. You like to think you helped the star and had no effect on the other. But I guess that's not really so. They're both my kids."

The basketball coaches at Hempstead High School kept a close watch over Ryan's program. When a boy turned thirteen, he entered the eighth grade and was eligible to play on the freshman team. In most Long Island communities freshman ball is the first organized ball a kid gets to play. But Ryan's team gave the kids and coaches at Hempstead the advantage of some earlier experience. Ryan even modeled his team after the high school team, having his boys play the same style ball and run the same plays.

Coach Ollie Mills couldn't wait to get his hands on the boys from that 31-and-1 team of Ryan's. "As a rule, Long Island public schools are only competitive among each other," Mills said. "But with Al Williams and Erving we could have had the best team in the state and maybe even the country."

But during the summer, before Julius was to enter the eighth grade, his mother married a man named Lindsay and moved her family into his house on Pleasant Avenue in Roosevelt. That was 1964 and the town of Hempstead had just completed the park in Roosevelt. And Julius Erving's feats in the park would do for Roosevelt what Schlitz beer claims it did for Milwaukee.

As winter approached, Julius tried out for the freshman team at Roosevelt Junior High. The coach was a man named Earl Moseley, a special-education teacher at the school. Moseley watched the transfer student for one day and knew he had something special. He promptly notified Ray Wilson and Charles McIllwain, the coac' at the high school, that he had a boy they had to see. And he sat down with Mrs. Lindsay and explained to her that her son was a rare talent and he was going to spend a lot of time after school making sure he made the best use of that talent.

Earl Moseley, a small, thin man of forty-three with gray spots throughout his Afro, is now the principal of the Theodore Roosevelt Elementary School. His office there is still cluttered with scrapbooks filled with clippings describing Julius' accomplishments. On his bulletin board is a picture of the star in his Nets uniform.

"Julius was never a street hanger," he says. "He would never hang out drinking wine like so many of the other kids did. If you wanted Julius, you always knew where to find him—in the park or at school.

"It wasn't long before Jewel—that's what we called him then—owned that park. Everyone wanted to play against him. Especially the older and bigger kids.

"He never asserted himself by being brash or loud or lewd. And I never remember seeing him in a fight or an argument. And you gotta know that many of the games in that park ended in fights or arguments. Most of the kids wanted to show they were the best with their fists.

"But Jewel always asserted himself by creating a move."

When Julius entered the ninth grade, high school coach, Ray Wilson wanted him to play on the junior varsity. But Moseley told him the kid was still rough and needed another year of freshman ball.

"That was a real con job," Wilson says. Moseley just wanted his star back for another season.

As a sophomore he did play on the junior varsity. He was better than most of the kids on the varsity, but Wilson believes strongly in giving the upper-classmen a chance to play; Julius would get a lot more playing time on the junior varsity.

With two games left in the season Wilson did bring

Julius up to the varsity. And with a few minutes left in the last game at West Hempstead High School, he put him in.

He promptly showed the folks at West Hempstead what he had been doing on the playgrounds in Roosevelt. He took a pass down near the basket in the low post, dribbled under the basket, and laid the ball up and in, untouched.

Earl Moseley was sitting next to Wilson on the Roosevelt bench. He gave the coach a shot in the arm and said, "Didn't he?"

Wilson just shook his head and said, "He did."

As a junior, Julius was obviously the best kid on the Roosevelt team. But Wilson didn't start him. Instead he started five hardnosed, burly seniors. "Julius is of the nature that he will do whatever is necessary to win at the expense of individual glory," Wilson says. "All kids aren't like this. So as a coach you try to take advantage of the ones who are. I knew he could come off the bench and handle it, while some of the others could not."

Still, Julius led the team in scoring, averaging 18 points a game, and also in rebounding. The team finished with 13 wins and 4 losses and was eliminated in the first round of the county playoffs.

Julius was six-feet-two then, and Wilson moved him back and forth between center and guard. So he was learning the necessities of two different positions at an early stage in his career.

* * *

Ray Wilson is now an assistant basketball coach at the University of Massachusetts. His main responsibility is recruiting high school talent. I caught up with him on a day in February when he was back on Long Island scouting talent. He sat in a coffee shop in Rockville Centre, drinking black coffee, very interested in being a part of any project that dealt with Julius.

He is a tall, handsome, well-dressed black man who

once had dreams of being a pro basketball player himself. But somewhere between three colleges and the army, that dream got messed up and he ended up teaching and coaching at Roosevelt in 1958.

"The strange thing about athletics," he told me, "is that as a kid you start out with a dream and you try to obtain that dream at a price of excluding everything else in your life. I ignored my social life and academics for basketball. At Xavier University in New Orleans the academics caught up with me and I became disillusioned. So I didn't work as hard at my dream anymore and I lost much of my ability.

"But you mature and you begin to rationalize and you say to yourself, 'This game's been good to me so let me go into coaching.' You become a coach and you hope that someday a kid crosses your path who will have some effect on the game of basketball. And when you find that kid, you start the old dream all over again.

"That's what Julius was to me. I lived my own dream through him.

"I always got a lot of pleasure out of talking to Julius. He never had to dominate a situation, so he was never a threat to anybody. He has that inner security. That made it easy for people of lesser talent to play with him and people who didn't play the game to be friends with him.

"And when you had something to say to him, the best approach was, 'Hey, man, I feel this . . .' and let it go. You never say to Julius, 'You should do this.' He doesn't need that.

"But watching him was like being in the presence of a great painter and seeing him create something new for you each day.

"He let my dream continue along. I guess I can say, 'I didn't make it but my son did.' But with all the sons I had in high school, I guess the odds were in my favor."

Long Island is not known as a breeding ground for

athletes. Jimmy Brown and Matt Snell had played football in Nassau County. And Larry Brown and Artie Heyman had played basketball there. But getting recognition as a high school basketball player was like trying to get recognition as a stage actor in Des Moines.

After his junior year ended, Julius might have been the most talented secret in all of basketball. The best basketball was city basketball. No one would know Julius as long as he stayed out in the comfortable local parks.

During that summer, two boys from the city moved out to Roosevelt. George Green came from Queens and Tommy Taylor from Brooklyn. Green was six-feet-six and Taylor was six-feet-three. They would both be entering their junior year at Roosevelt.

They met Julius in the Roosevelt playgrounds. They told all their friends in the city about him. They brought Julius to the city to play against the best. The legend of Julius Erving started spreading beyond the hurricane fences of the Long Island playgrounds. City boys heard about him and they wanted to take him on. Soon the court at Roosevelt Park that was reserved for the better players was full of carpetbaggers. The local kids stood on the sidelines watching Erving, Green, and Taylor against all the kids from the city. And the park began to gain a reputation as a site for the best pickup games, a reputation usually reserved for places like Manhattan Beach. And fans flocked there like prospectors at Sutter's Mill.

School started. It got too cold to play in the park. And the beginning of basketball practice came around. With only Julius on his side, Ray Wilson thought he would have a good team. Now with Green and Taylor also, he had a cornucopia.

"Each one of them had some talent that was more unique than the other's," Wilson said. "If I needed a shooter, I would have taken George. If I needed a worker who would kill himself to make you a winner, I would have taken Tommy. And if I wanted the complete, all-around player, I would have taken Julius."

Julius had grown to six-feet-four by then, but there was still the question of how big he would be. If he reached six-feet-seven he was not only a college prospect, but a pro prospect. But Green was six-feet-six already, and he became the team's top college prospect. The scouts came out to see the team, looked at George's size on the lineup sheet, and knew he was their man.

The team started the season by winning its first 8 games. Julius was scoring more than 20 points a game, and Green and Taylor each had their high-scoring nights. They were all relaxed and having a good time winning.

There was one minor incident. The only one Wilson can ever remember having with Julius. He had scheduled a scrimmage at Levittown Memorial on an afternoon when the students were let out of school early. The bus was scheduled to leave at eleven and Julius jumped into a car with a bunch of friends to get some lunch. They were not back when the bus was set to leave so Wilson went ahead without them. Julius drove to the scrimmage, but Wilson didn't let him play. He thought it was an opportunity to discipline one of his stars and let everyone else on the team know Julius had the same rules they did.

Two years later Wilson was sitting around talking with some of his graduated players and it came out that they were late because they had stopped to help a teacher dig his car out of the snow. Julius had never mentioned it.

Hempstead had also won their first eight ball games, even without Julius on their team. Al Williams, Julius' Salvation Army teammate, was the star of that team, even though he was only five-feet-nine. The two teams met on a January Friday night at Hempstead; the home team embarrassed the visitor 81–61.

After that, both teams continued to win. Hempstead won 7 more in a row and were 16 and 0, the number-one-rated team in Nassau County. Roosevelt lost only one more game, to Long Beach, and were 14 and 2. Williams and Erving were recognized as the area's two best public school players, and scouts from all the major basketball schools were following their every move.

They met again on a Tuesday in February. At Roosevelt this time. Both had clinched a berth in the county playoffs. But this was an emotional match-up, a game between two schools that emphasized basketball in an area where wrestling was the more prestigious sport. A game between kids who had grown up playing with and against each other on the same playgrounds. A game between two predominantly black schools situated among white commuter communities. It was the closest thing to city ball that Long Island had seen in a long time.

Hempstead led the first quarter. Roosevelt led the second and it was close at the half. But Erving picked up his fourth personal foul early in the third quarter and had to sit down. Still, at the end of the third quarter the game was tied at 57. Hempstead threw the ball away a few times in the final period, Julius controlled the backboards and Roosevelt won 78–70. Julius finished with 22 points and 17 rebounds. Williams had 27 points. At the buzzer the fans poured out of the stands, which lined one side of the school's gym, like a waterfall. They had seen what might have been the best game in the history of Nassau County basketball.

Wilson was convinced he had the best team in the county. They finished 16 and 2 and easily defeated West Hempstead 82–48 in the first round of the playoffs. Julius scored 28 in that game and had 11 rebounds. In the

locker room Ray Wilson was surrounded by a crowd of
men. Not reporters. Recruiters.

But four days later Roosevelt fell apart and bowed to
Elmont Memorial, 62–49. Julius scored 19, but everyone
else had an off night. Wilson felt the refs should have
taken the night off, too.

"That game really disillusioned me," he said. "We
were the black team and there weren't too many others
on the Island. I sincerely believe we suffered at the
hands of the refs because of that."

The competition among the high schools was over for
the year. And the competition among the colleges began.
The four most sought-after kids on the Island were
Erving and Williams and two kids from parochial
schools—Bill Chamberlain from Lutheran and Tom Riker
from St. Dominic's, who because of his size (six-feet-
ten) was the most intensely recruited of all. The Atlantic
Coast Conference, the best basketball conference in the
country, managed to corral Riker for South Carolina
and Chamberlain for North Carolina.

Williams had close to one hundred offers early in his
senior year, but he had his own doubts about his size
and was thinking of attending a smaller school, Centen-
ary or East Tennessee State. But a few nights before
Hempstead was to play Elmont in the semifinal round of
the county playoffs, Williams was thrown out of a girls'
sports night at the school for flashing a bottle of wine
and showing that he had finished what was inside. Mills
was forced to suspend his best player for the rest of the
playoffs.

One by one, the offers from the colleges were revoked.
All but those from Laurinburg Institute, a small two-
year school in North Carolina and from little Pershing
College in Nebraska. So he went to Laurinburg. And
after completing his two years there, one of his sociology
professors wrote to Niagara University in Buffalo to tell
them about Williams. He went on to lead Niagara to the

finals of the National Invitation Tournament and continued there until he earned his master's degree in penology.

Early in his senior year, Julius visited schools all over the country. He visited places as big as the University of Iowa, where Connie Hawkins had started, and as small as Cleveland State University. But he soon decided that he wanted to stay within reasonable distance of home. His brother, Marvin, was sick, suffering from a rare skin disease called *lupus erythematosus*. His sister, Alexis, was planning to get married and leave town. Julius wanted to be close to his mother and also to the people he had come to depend on, people like Ryan and Moseley and Wilson.

So he visited New York schools. Manhattan. St. Johns.

He want to visit Hofstra in Hempstead and was shown around the campus by Barry White, the star of their basketball team. White brought him into the Rathskeller to talk to a few of the guys. There he met a fellow named Dave Brownbill. Brownbill had averaged 28 points a game as a guard for Hofstra in the beginning of the season and was being scouted by the pros. But Coach Paul Lynner moved him to forward and his whole game fell apart. Brownbill was disgusted and he told Julius he was better off not coming to Hofstra and playing for Lynner. Julius appreciated the honesty.

He was also seriously considering schools in Massachusetts: Boston University, where Ray Wilson had completed school, and the University of Massachusetts, where Wilson's former college teammate Jack Leaman was the coach.

"As much time as you spend with your boys during the years they play for you," Wilson said, "you never get as close to them as when they are being recruited by colleges. That's when they start to depend on you for advice and protection. That's when you stop being a coach and start being a father. And so you gotta be careful and make sure you're not just acting out your dream and sending him to UCLA or North Carolina, where every youngster dreams of going. You got to make sure that he goes where it's good for him."

Wilson spent much of his time that year protecting Julius. He wanted to avoid creating the circus of lies and bribes that so often surrounds recruitment. He requested that all interested recruiters deal through him.

"So many kids go away to college as major talents and become monsters," Wilson says. "The only thing a coach could hope for is that they'll treat your kid like a man. You don't ask for any favors. You just want him to get a chance to play and learn. So your best bet is guiding him somewhere where you know the coach."

Julius narrowed his choices down to St. Johns University, a local but accomplished basketball school in Jamaica, New York, and the University of Massachusetts, a rural, campus school, without much of a reputation for big-time sports, but where Wilson's friend Leaman was the coach.

"All along I kept telling myself that I wasn't going to make the decision for him," Wilson says. "He would just nod his head as if he was telling me I was going to make it if he could con me into it. The beauty of the whole thing is I still don't know if I made it for him."

Julius entered the University of Massachusetts in September of 1968.

He was entering a school where he would not benefit from the high-powered publicity campaigns of the major basketball schools. A school where he could do more for their program than their program could do for him.

But Julius didn't worry about those things. He didn't need the prestige of an Atlantic Coast or Big Ten school lettered across his uniform. He had too much self-confidence to be concerned with that. It was more important for him to stay close to the people who had helped him develop that maturity. He might stay obscure, but he would be secure.

4. Hiding Out in Amherst

The National College Athletic Association, the governing body of college sports, divides its member schools into two groups—small college and major college. But within the major-college grouping there are at least three levels of basketball competition.

At the highest level are the teams in the Atlantic Coast Conference, the Big Ten Conference, the Pacific Coast Conference and a large number of independent schools such as Marquette and South Carolina and Notre Dame, which hire big-name coaches and publicize their programs tirelessly. The finalists on the NCAA's annual championship tournament almost always come from this level. And year after year, schools from this group hold the top rankings in the two national wire-service polls. These schools have the highest-financed, most flamboyant, and usually the most ruthless recruiting programs.

The middle level includes the Ivy League, the Southeast Conference, the Southwest Conference, the Middle American Conference, the Missouri Valley Conference, the Big Eight Conference, the Western Athletic Conference, and a number of independents such as Cincinnati and Jacksonville and Niagara. These schools usually manage to squeeze a few teams into the top twenty in the national polls and occasionally their teams manage to break through and make the national semifinals.

The lowest level includes the Yankee Conference, of which Massachusetts is a member, the Big Sky Conference, the Southern Conference, a bunch of small obscure conferences, and a host of independent schools. Most of these schools recruit only regionally. They usually get knocked out in the first round of the NCAA tournament. And a couple of them can sneak into the polls, usually by running up an impressive number of wins against impotent opponents.

There are times when these levels change slightly. An independent school gains an outstanding player who gets national attention. Or a conference happens to have two or three good teams at the same time and can rise, as the Ivy League did when it had strong teams at Penn and Princeton or the Southern Conference when Jerry West was at West Virginia. But eventually it all evens out and the teams and leagues return to their respective levels.

When Julius Erving chose to go to the University of Massachusetts, he was getting in on the lowest level. He was certainly capable of competing against any of his contemporaries at such top-level schools as UCLA, North Carolina, or Ohio State. But by choosing to enter U. Mass. he accepted the limitations on the national recognition his team would receive and, consequently, the attention he would receive.

U. Mass., he accepted the limitations on the national wooded, quaint town of Amherst, about one hundred miles from the excitement of Boston. The design and setting of the school speak out to tell you it is a loner, operating relaxed by itself away from the academic competition of the Hub's great schools. In June, 1968, all schools had closed abruptly after the shooting of Bobby Kennedy. And the leisure of summer had been interrupted by the horrors of the 1968 Democratic Party Convention in Chicago, which appeared on the television in every living room. The effects of those events would pull the emotions of all college campuses together so that no setting was away from it all. Everyplace was part of it.

Like the very setting he chose to live in, Julius himself was a loner. Most of the people living in the South Shore Long Island communities near Roosevelt lived there because it was an easy commute to New York City. Commuters went to the city each day to work and on weekends to be entertained. Julius had gone to the city only to play basketball. And at the playground in Roosevelt he managed to ignore the Big Apple's other influences. So he was immediately comfortable in the rural hush of Amherst.

Moseley and Wilson had made him realize early that basketball could mean something very special to him. That there was a lot of pleasure and comfort the game could bring him if he worked at it. And as soon as he arrived at U. Mass., he immersed himself in it. When he arrived, he was a rough playground player. He was a poor outside shooter. But he realized his limitation. In the late-summer heat of September he would go down to the gym in the Boyden Building, the men's physical-education center, and work on his game. It was ninety degrees inside and you couldn't wear anything but shorts. But Julius would work for hours by himself. Soon the word got out that there was a new performer, a new artist in the gym, and the bleachers would be filled with fifty or sixty people sitting in the heat each day watching him take hundreds of shots.

In October freshman practice began. Julius had grown an inch and a half over the summer and was now six-feet-four and a half. He could handle the ball like a smaller man and rebound like a bigger man. So Coach Jack Leaman instructed Pete Broker, his freshman coach, to play him at both guard and forward just as Ray Wilson had. That lasted about three games. Both men realized Julius was the best rebounder they had ever had at U. Mass. And so he was put at forward and played in as close to the basket as possible. The Redmen coaches used a team-oriented game that emphasized defense and set plays on offense. They did not change this style for Julius. Rather than adopting a wide-open run and shoot, schoolyard attack, they asked him to learn the discipline of their theories. He adjusted quickly.

The team was winning. And the school was excited about it. Freshman games began at six. But the lineup for seats began forming in front of the Curry Hicks Cage, at three. The varsity had their best season ever, winning 18 and losing 6. But all the talk was about the freshman team. The undefeated freshman team—16 and 0. Led by Julius Erving, who broke the freshman records for scoring and rebounding.

By season's end Julius was the biggest name on the campus. He dug into the books and anticipated next year's basketball season. Then in the spring he was summoned home suddenly. Marvin had died.

"I cried all day on the day of the funeral," Julius said. "I went to the cemetery the first two days after he was buried and I cried each day. Then I went the next day and I didn't cry. I told myself I wasn't going to cry anymore. I haven't cried over anything since that day in 1969, and I don't know what it would take to make me cry again. I don't have any fears. I'm not afraid of dying. That traumatic experience changed my life."

Julius came home for the summer to be with his mother and took a job with the town of Hempstead running Roosevelt Park. He had the keys to the playground. It was his responsibility to shut off the lights and lock up when the park closed. But he would stay around after everyone else was gone and work on his own game.

In September Julius returned to U. Mass. for his sophomore year. But he was aware of a player named Spencer Haywood, who did not return to his school, Detroit University, but instead signed a contract with the Denver Rockets of the American Basketball Association. He was not yet twenty; he had completed only two years of college. And he was being paid $250,000 a year.

Joining Julius at U. Mass. was his high school coach,
Ray Wilson. He had decided to leave Roosevelt and accept a job as assistant to his friend Jack Leaman.

It looked as if Wilson delivered Julius to Leaman just
as Robert Vesco delivered campaign money to Nixon.
Such occurrences are not uncommon. In the dogfight for
Lew Alcindor his high school coach, Jack Donohue, was
awarded the head coaching job at Holy Cross, a school
Alcindor eventually rejected in favor of UCLA. And
when Jerry West graduated from the University of West
Virginia and joined the Lakers, his college coach, Fred
Schaus, became the Lakers coach. But there is much
more to Ray Wilson's story than the delivery of a package. He is a gentle, warm man who was very dedicated
to his kids at Roosevelt. And he would not have given
up that personal gratification to do college recruiting
merely for the prestige of being associated with a
college.

The year after Julius graduated from Roosevelt, Green
and Taylor led the team to a great start. With 3 games
left they had only 1 loss and were rated first in the
county. But one afternoon Wilson received a phone call
from someone in Springfield Gardens in Queens, where
Green had begun his schooling, informing him that
George was actually nineteen years old. New York State
rules forbid anyone to complete in high school athletics
after the age of eighteen. Roosevelt was forced to forfeit all the games they had won, and Green's high school
basketball career was over.

"This was the worst thing that had ever happened to
me as a coach," Wilson says. "I now know that I should
have allowed George Green to continue to play even if
it cost me my job outright. When something is your
whole world as a kid, what right does some adult have
to take it away from you if you're not hurting anyone.

"You have to know George to understand. Basketball
was his whole life."

The incident was the beginning of a tough few years for Green. Despite his size and ability the colleges that were chasing him seemed less interested after he was dropped from the Roosevelt team. And he settled for an obscure two-year school in Florida. After finishing up there, he transferred to Parsons College in Iowa. But Parsons soon went bankrupt and George went home. He tried desperately to get into a school somewhere else but had no success. He ended up jobless in New York, supporting himself on the little money he made playing in the Eastern League and pickup games around the city.

Between this incident and the loss to Elmont the year before (in which Wilson felt his team had been mistreated) Wilson was ready to turn his back on high school ball.

Then on June 28, his wedding anniversary, he took his wife to New York City to celebrate. When they returned to their Deer Park home, they discovered they had been robbed. The place was a mess. About $5,000 worth of jewelry and clothes and odds and ends was missing.

"After growing up poor your whole life and finally being able to acquire some things, it's a big blow when something like this happens," Wilson says. "And it's scary knowing that someone else out there knows your house as well as you do."

That was the final blow. Wilson decided to pack up and take the job Jack Leaman had been offering him for years before either of them had even known who Julius Erving was.

"Sure I knew that once he hit the headlines there would be talk that I was clinging to Julius' coattails," he says. "But I knew that the people who knew me wouldn't even ask for an explanation. Maybe I learned a little about inner security from Julius."

That year U. Mass. had a team made up of seniors who the year before had been the core of the best team the school had ever had and sophomores who had been the core of the best freshman team the school had ever had. In the beginning of the year they had trouble playing together and they won only half of their first dozen games. But then they discovered each other's talents and won 13 straight.

In one game, against Boston University, Julius scored 29 points and had 20 rebounds in the first half. The school record at the time was 41 points and 28 rebounds in a game.

He came out in the second half, stopped shooting and picked up 15 assists. He finished the night with 34 points and tied the record for rebounds.

Leaman could not understand why his sophomore had stopped shooting. After the game he called Julius aside and said, "If I play you in a game, I want you to play, not fool around."

"If I broke those records here tonight," Julius said, "what would I have to shoot for in the next two years?"

U. Mass. finished the season with 18 wins and 7 losses and was invited to the National Invitation Tournament at Madison Square Garden. In the first round they were matched up against Marquette University, the first seed. Marquette was rated second in the national polls behind UCLA. They were invited to the NCAA championship tournament but were asked to compete in the tougher Midwest regional instead of the Mideast, where they belonged. Coach Al McGuire thought his team was being taken advantage of and turned down the NCAA bid for the NIT. His team defeated Massachusetts by 5 points and then went on to win the tournament easily.

As impressive as Julius was wherever he played, he had always faced competition considered less than the best. Despite his heroics, this tarnished the legend. But in the summer between his sophomore and junior years of college, two events helped remove some of that tarnish.

The NCAA was sending a team of the best American

college players to tour Europe and Russia. Jack Leaman had tried to get Julius an invitation to try out for that team at a camp at the Air Force Academy in Colorado Springs, but the organizers were not interested in someone from a school like U. Mass. even if he averaged 26 points a game and was second in the nation in rebounding. So Julius went off to spend the early part of the summer teaching at an instructional camp in Indiana.

Then one morning, at four A.M., Leaman got a telephone call at home telling him to send Julius out there. "I'll never forget that they called me at four A.M.," he says.

He called Julius first thing the next morning and he was in Colorado the same night. He went on to make the team and to win the award as the most valuable player on the tour. "That was a turning point in his career," Leaman says. "Then he knew that no matter how much recognition U. Mass. had or didn't have he was as great as any college player in the country."

After the tour was over he returned home to Roosevelt and to pickup games in the parks. One day Dave Brownbill called and asked Julius to accompany him to Richie O'Connor Park on Hillside Avenue in Queens, where there was supposed to be a hot pickup game between some pros and some college players.

They got to the park and discovered that Em Bryant, Nate Bowman, and Dave Stallworth, all of them New York Knicks, were playing on the pro team.

"The match up was Julius against Stallworth," Brownbill says. "And early on, Julius made a move out of the corner, went past Dave, and dunked.

"Then he came right back and went the other way and dunked again. Dave was getting pissed off. He started to lean on Julius and push him around. But whenever he leaned on him, Julius just rolled the other way and easily went to the hoop.

"The two of them played to a standoff. The big star

from the world-champion Knicks. And the college kid from some unknown small school. That day Julius found out how good he was."

A few weeks later Brownbill went to a party at the house of Sonny Dove. Dove was an All-American at St. John's who was never able to make it in the pros. His game was confined to the schoolyard. "All the talk that night was about this kid Juluis," Brownbill recalls, "and how he was making all the pros look bad in the parks."

That summer Brownbill had moved to Roosevelt and he used to meet up with Julius around the park all the time. "I remember he had this old beat-up Chevy at the time. I used to see him every time I passed a gas station. He was always having some kind of trouble with it. I told him he'd be better off if someone stole the car.

"Well, one night he came home from an all-star game he had played in and left the trophies he had won in the back seat of his car. The next morning he came out and the car was gone. They probably wanted the trophies. If they weren't in there, the car wouldn't have been stolen. The trophies were worth more than the car."

In September Julius returned to U. Mass. for his junior year. But another junior, Ralph Simpson, did not return to the University of Michigan for his. Instead, he signed a contract with the Denver Rockets. He would be paid $250,000 a year for three years, $750,000 in mutual funds and $35,000 a year after he reached the age of forty.

At the same time Spencer Haywood was renegotiating with the Rockets. But he was not satisfied and instead accepted an offer from the Seattle Supersonics of the National Basketball Association for $1.5 million for six years. The NBA had a rule forbidding owners to sign an undergraduate until his college class had graduated. When they heard of Haywood's signing, they voted 15–2 to throw Sam Schulman, the owner of the Sonics, out of the League. But Schulman went to court and had the so-called four-year rule declared illegal. Haywood was his property. And warfare between the two pro leagues, which until then had been confined to graduating seniors, would have new boundaries. It was hell for the owners. It was utopia for the college players.

At the same time that tumult was erupting in pro basketball, tumult was erupting on the college campuses. U. Mass. had erupted in violence set off by a racial dispute in 1968, Julius' freshman year. And the blacks took an active role in the campus activity again in 1971. But Julius refused to make a commitment. He was the best-known black on campus. But his popularity came from playing basketball. He had no interest in using his influence anywhere else. Leaman says he likes to think that in a time of crisis, the basketball team acted as a unifying force.

Ignoring the campus problems, the team got off to a great start, but then lost two in a row to Providence and Springfield, each by one point. In the Providence game, Julius blew a four-foot layup at the buzzer. A few years later, he told Leaman the one thing that stuck in his mind about his college career was that layup.

Late in the season, with 20 wins already and a sure tournament berth of some kind coming their way, Massachusetts met my school, George Washington University, in Madison Square Garden. GWU was a minor basketball school, a dropout of the Southern Conference, and, like U. Mass., on the lowest level of big-colleges.

Even though there were members of both teams who were taller, the entire area within eight or nine feet of the basket belonged to Julius. He went over the defenders and around them, scoring at will, rebounding with authority. He finished the day with 35 points and 17 rebounds and U. Mass. beat GWU 70–65.

I was not the only one to have revived my love affair with this major talent. The next day the New York press took the opportunity to sing the local boy's praises. There were only a few thousand people scattered in the

Garden, the largest major basketball arena in the country. But by Sunday millions more knew about Julius' impressive performance. A show like that at a place like the Garden was what was needed to focus attention on someone who had hidden out in Roosevelt and Amherst all his life.

The team lost one more regular-season game to a good Fordham team and finished the year with a record of 23 wins and 3 losses, the best in the school's history.

Leaman hoped that the recognition that Julius had received would gain his team a bid to the NCAA Eastern regionals. But that bid never came. And so they returned to the NIT. They got by their first-round opponent but then faced North Carolina, the top-seeded team, in the second round. They were down by 11 points with nineteen minutes left in the game when Julius fouled out. The team fell apart and ended up losing by 41 points. North Carolina even managed to score 4 points with only one second remaining on the clock. Leaman said it was the longest afternoon he ever had to sit through. And he was glad to get out of town quickly to attend the NCAA coaches' meeting in Houston.

While the college players were completing their tournament play, the owners of the ABA franchises were holding a league meeting. It was still weeks before the draft would be held. But Earl Foreman, the owner of the Virginia Squires, wanted the rights to sign the junior from Massachusetts.

Mike Storen was at that meeting representing the Kentucky Colonels. "When Foreman asked for the rights to this kid, I remember thinking to myself, 'Who cares?'" he says. "I told Foreman if he wanted him, he should go sign him.

"Roy Boe [owner of the New York Nets] started asking Foreman if the kid's name was Erving or Irvine, they started bickering back and forth, and all the other owners started screaming to forget it so they could go on with their business and catch their flights home."

So Foreman left that meeting with the rights to sign Julius if he could. An attorney named Steve Arnold contacted Julius, said he was representing the ABA and said there were teams interested in signing him if he were ready to give up school. Julius was not yet sure. But when he went home for Easter vacation, he stopped in at the Nets offices in Carle Place to ask if they wanted to sign him. Boe was on vacation in Florida, but Lou Carnesecca, the Nets coach and general manager was in the office. Carnesecca had been the coach at St. John's when Julius was deciding whether to go there or to U. Mass. Carnesecca lost him that time and regretted it. He didn't want to lose him again. He promptly put through a call to Boe and told him that Julius Erving was standing there in the office ready to sign. Boe said that morally he was very much against signing underclassmen and turned down the opportunity. Carnesecca was heartbroken. He knew someone else would grab at the opportunity.

While Julius was bartering his talents, Jack Leaman was attending the meetings planned around the finals of the NCAA tournament at the Astrodome in Houston. "A bunch of coaches were joking around and saying that the ABA was signing undergraduates," Leaman recalls. "I kind of laughed along with them. I knew I wouldn't be affected. The pros never looked at New England ballplayers. Especially when they were only juniors."

The next morning the phone rang in Leaman's hotel room. It was Ray Wilson. His voice was soft and sad. He said something was brewing and Leaman better hurry home. He got on the next plane to Boston, and that night Julius told him he was planning to go to Philadelphia to meet with Foreman.

"I was in a real bind," Leaman said. "It was the first

time I was ever in that situation, and I didn't know how
to handle it.

"At first I was amazed and bitter. I had put together
a club, my best club, and they were entering their senior
year, when they should have peaked. And someone was
trying to bust it up."

But Leaman quickly realized it was his responsibility
to help Julius as much as possible. He contacted a friend
named Ronnie Perry, who then put him in touch with
Bob Woolf, the Boston-based attorney who had a reputation as the most trustworthy of all the agents negotiating
for athletes. "I figured he had such a big reputation that
he couldn't afford to cheat my kid," Leaman said.

On April 6, Julius, Ray Wilson, and Woolf went to
Philadelphia and met with Earl Foreman. That day
Julius signed a contract that would pay him $500,000
over a period of four years.

"I realized that in all honesty," Erving said, "my main
preference was playing basketball. Going to college was
a secondary thing. It would have been stupid for me to
deny myself that financial opportunity."

"Now that I look back over the whole situation," Leaman says, "I realize that he made the right move at the
time. He had gotten as much out of college ball as he
could have gotten.

"I think when he was here, we did what turned out to
be best for him. We made him play team defense and
team offense. He could have scored a lot more, but we
gave him a better understanding of the game. We set it
up so that he could handle a lot of situations he would
face in the pros, situations that many college hotshots
had trouble handling.

"I divided my salary into what they offered Julius and
I figured out that it would take me thirty-eight years to
earn what he was getting for four. I knew I couldn't
argue with him then."

It would have taken Leaman his whole lifetime, maybe two, to earn what some of the other college kids were signing for at the same time.

George McGinnis, a nineteen-year-old sophomore at Indiana University, signed with the Indiana Pacers for $60,000 a year for three years, a $45,000 bonus, a $10,000 grant to finish college, $250 a month rent for an apartment, $20,000 to buy three cars, and a retirement annuity after age forty of $40,000 a year.

At the same time Ken Durrett from LaSalle signed with the Cincinnati Royals for $1.5 million; Johnny Neumann, a sophomore at the University of Mississippi, signed with the Memphis Tams for $2 million; Jim Mc-Daniels from Western Kentucky signed with the Carolina Cougars for $2.9 million; Sidney Wicks from UCLA signed with the NBA Portland Trail Blazers for $1.5 million; Artis Gilmore of Jacksonville University signed with the Kentucky Colonels for $2.2 million; Austin Carr from Notre Dame signed with the Cleveland Cavaliers for $1.4 million; Elmore Smith from an obscure school called Kentucky State signed with the Buffalo Braves for $1.8 million; and Howard Porter from Villanova signed with the Pittsburgh Condors for $1 million.

The war between the NBA and the ABA had gotten completely out of hand. They were spending as much as they had to sign whomever they could. Draft rights were ignored. The only rules were there were no rules. There were only three or four teams in all of basketball that were making any kind of profit at the time. It was obvious that this insanity could not go on forever. So Julius had made the only decision that any rational, intelligent person could make. Especially any rational person whose mother had had to do day work to supplement her welfare check to be able to feed her family. He was turning pro and getting a lot of money. Only the pro team was in Norfolk, which was not a pro city. And the lot of money was a lot less than any other much-sought-after rookie was getting paid. Despite his talent, it appeared that his obscurity was beginning to catch up with Doctor J.

5. The Other Leagues

To the middle-class American, television-watching sports audience, basketball happens in modern, sterile, air-conditioned arenas between October and May. But for the kids who grow up in and around the city playgrounds, who spend ten hours a hot summer day there, who shoot the ball into corrugated-metal garbage cans when the courts are full, and who have rheumatoid knees from the time they are eighteen because of the pouncing on the cement, basketball happens on asphalt, cyclone-fenced playgrounds between June and August.

The summer leagues. The Rucker in New York. The Baker in Philly. And similar leagues in Washington, Los Angeles, Indianapolis, and Chicago. To their audience any game there is as important as any pro playoff. If the playoffs are pro ball's second season, then summer ball is the third season.

In the summer of 1971, with a contract worth a half-million dollars tucked in his jock, Julius Erving played summer ball. Pete Vecsey, a writer who covered pro basketball for the *Daily News*, was organizing a team called the Westsiders in the Rucker tournament. Billy Paultz and Ollie Taylor from the New York Nets joined the team. So did Charlie Scott, who would be Julius' teammate on the Virginia Squires. And Julius and Dave Brownbill, still living at home on Long Island. Spending time together on the basketball court in the summer had made Julius and Dave the closest of friends. The Rucker was probably the only competitive situation in which they could be teammates.

The summer leagues usually feature four classifications of ballplayers: the college stars who have ambitions of playing pro ball and come here to see how good they are; the graduated college players who never quite made it in the pros, now play in such semi-pro leagues as the Eastern League and hope to get another pro try-out; the guys who will never be pros and come to the court to show the stars how tough they really are; and the pros who though they are wealthy haven't forgotten their ghetto roots and whose knees are strong enough to take the extra punishment after the hundred-game season.

Everyone in the playground has something to prove. Something individual. And so winning becomes less important than embarrassing your opponent. And passing to the open man becomes less important than wiggling around five or six players for your own shot. Instead of two teams of five men, summer leagues are ten individuals against each other. Julius was bred on this kind of ball. Despite the discipline he had learned at U. Mass., he was still the ultimate playground player.

The Rucker games are usually played on Saturday and Sunday afternoons on the Holcombe Rucker Playground in Harlem. But on the day the Westsiders were scheduled to play their first game it rained. So the game was moved indoors to a high school gym. The playground is said to be able to hold 5,000 people and that's probably an exaggeration. But that day enough fans to fill it showed up. The gym holds only 1,000. And so they let the crowd in in shifts while the others stood out in the rain and waited. They would stop the game at the end of the quarter and let in a whole new crowd of people.

On the first play of that game Julius got the ball between three players who were bigger than he was—Sid Catlett from Notre Dame, Marv Roberts from Utah

State, and a guy named Jim Reed. Julius wiggled out from between the three of them and slam dunked. The roof nearly fell in. Vecsey was standing on the sidelines slapping five with everybody in the first row. The place was buzzing.

It didn't take long for word about this new sensation to get out. The Rucker gets minimal coverage in the New York papers. The excitement is created strictly by word of mouth. When word got out that the Doctor was coming, the playground would fill up hours in advance of game time.

Julius used to drive to the games from Long Island with Dave Brownbill. "We would arrive at the crowded court," Dave says, "and the mob would part like the waters of the Red Sea. I got identified with the Doctor, and if I ever arrived without him, I got booed.

"He averaged forty-five points a game that summer and he was blocking shots all over the place. Even when he threw the ball away he got a standing ovation.

"Our team got into a rut that I like to call court tilt. We all wanted to see Julius do his thing. So we all went to one side of the basket and left him alone on the other. It was fun to watch him, but you don't win too many that way.

"By the time he left the Rucker that summer he felt he was ready for the pros. He realized that he would be able to do the same kinds of things up there that he did against kids his own age."

So after the summer Julius Erving went off to rookie camp with the Virginia Squires. And his friend, Dave Brownbill, returned to his job working for the town of Hempstead Parks Department. On the weekends that Julius would be playing in modern arenas against such teams as Denver and San Diego and New York, Dave would be playing in high school gyms against Hartford and Scranton and Allentown and Trenton. He was a member of the Wilkes-Barre Barons of the Eastern League.

The Eastern League is made up mostly of players who live in and around New York and who drive through the rain and snow for hours to get to their Saturday and Sunday games. They get there and run up and down the court full speed in a game that is without defense and where the contact is worse than in the National Hockey League. It takes about 140 points to win, and both teams usually come very near to that mark. The players go through all this for about $100 a game. For his first season with Wilkes-Barre Brownbill got $50.

They play in any high school gym the franchise owner can weasel his way into for nothing or close to it. And they draw crowds you would expect to find at the roller derby.

Why do they do it?

Brownbill explains: "Stan Pollack, who played college ball at the University of Pennsylvania, once told me that when he first got out of school, he thought the Eastern League would get him into the pros. But after a while it just becomes a good way to make some money on weekends. When you're making $200 a week, another $200 on the weekend comes in handy."

A few players from the league have made it to the pros. Mike Riordan, now with the Baltimore Bullets, and Harthorne Wingo, now with the Knicks, both started out in the Eastern League. But far more players went the other way. Unable to make it with an NBA team, they were sent to the Eastern League to work on their games. They work on it until they reach change of life without hearing from the NBA.

"There are of course stars in the pro leagues who no one doubts belong there," Brownbill says. "But below that there are the hangers-on who now make good money because the game is inflated. The difference between the hangers-on and the Eastern League is usually only a matter of circumstance. A fight with a coach. Someone's eligibility problems. Someone else's personality. Things that get in the way of ability and determine where you end up."

Brownbill joined the Eastern League. And Julius joined the other league.

The "other league" is the American Basketball Association. Other than the National Basketball Association, which was established in 1947. Other not because of when it started, but because of where it started.

The formation of the American Basketball Association was announced at a news conference at the Carlyle Hotel in New York on February 2, 1966. It was the brainchild of a young California tax lawyer named Gary Davidson. He had seen the success the AFL had managed to achieve quickly, and as a basketball fan he saw no reason why a new league in his favorite sport could not do the same.

When he made the announcement, Davidson had a cast on his arm, the result of an accident that had occurred while playing basketball. He recruited as fellow owners other rich men who liked to play the game, men like Joe Gregory in Louisville and singer Pat Boone in Oakland. The AFL, after all, had been conceived by Lamar Hunt, the Dallas-based millionaire son of oil baron H. L. Hunt, and a football enthusiast who reportedly took part in his team's pass-catching drills during their early years. The men who invested in the ABA thought they could imitate the owners from the AFL and build themselves teams with which to practice. They also hoped to imitate the AFL's formula for success.

Unfortunately none of those men were from New York, Los Angeles, or Chicago. They started teams in Teaneck, New Jersey, Anaheim, California, and Indianapolis. But that's like sitting in the Brooklyn Paramount and watching Jean Harlow up on the screen and wanting to reach out and kiss her. So close and yet so far.

They also had teams in Pittsburgh, Minneapolis, Louisville, New Orleans, Denver, Dallas, Houston, and Oakland. Eleven teams but not one in the five most populated cities in the country.

In its formative stage, the ABA hired George Mikan as its first commissioner. Mikan had been the first superstar in the NBA when he played for the Minneapolis Lakers in the 1940's and 1950's. He remains popular, and his presence attracted more monied basketball fans to invest in the proposed franchises.

Mikan is also an innovative basketball mind. He designed three unique concepts that differentiated this league from the established league. He created a three-point basket awarded if a player made good on a shot from outside a semi-circle drawn on the court twenty-five feet from the basket; he adopted a rule requiring each team to shoot within 30 seconds of the time they took possession of the ball, six seconds more than are given to the teams in the NBA; and he designed a red, white, and blue basketball that was laughed at in the beginning but has since become the trademark of the ABA and the largest-selling promotional sports item of all time. (When the two leagues do merge, the red, white, and blue ball will surely be used.)

As the ABA entered its second season (which was one more than many people said it would ever have), New Jersey had moved to Long Island—which was farther from New York City than New Jersey—and began calling itself New York; Anaheim moved to Los Angeles; and Pittsburgh moved to Miami.

In that same year Pat Boone's Oakland Oaks persuaded Rick Barry, a handsome, blond glamor boy who was a rookie sensation with the National Basketball Association's San Francisco team, to jump across the bay and join their team. They also asked his father-in-law, Bruce Hale, to join them as general manager. In many families that would seem to be the worst possible means of persuasion; in this family, Barry claims, it made all the difference.

It had become a cliché in sportswriting that one charismatic player can make a league. That he can draw so much attention that people will take interest in the league as a whole and begin to appreciate the other players and the other teams. One athlete said to have accomplished this is Joe Namath, the quarterback for the New York Jets of the American Football League. Namath rose to the top of his own league and led his team to win over the Baltimore Colts, the champion of the established NFL, in the Super Bowl. The ABA hoped Rick Barry could do the same for them.

In his first season, Barry led the ABA in scoring and led his team to an easy championship. He dominated his league more than Namath ever had or ever would dominate his. But all Barry's accomplishments did was highlight the uniqueness of Namath and his situation. Barry's coming over from the established league, and his dominance, just showed the dominance of the established league's talent. Namath developed his talent within the upstart league and then rose up to defeat the established league. Barry played in Oakland, which has always asserted itself as one of the worst sports towns in America. Namath played in New York which is undoubtedly the best.

After his victory Namath was no longer thought of in the same terms as John Unitas or Bart Starr, the other champion quarterbacks. He was a celebrity, like Frank Sinatra or Mick Jagger. He was perhaps the best-known athlete in the world, with the possible exception of Muhammad Ali. Barry was still just a basketball star who couldn't even attract enough attention to assure his team's success in Oakland.

Before the third season began, Barry was out of Oakland, and George Mikan was out of his job.

Once the league began operating, Mikan found himself unable to cope with the administrative problems of running it. The owners no longer felt they needed a basketball name at the helm to legitimize them. Television had given the AFL the money to make it, and the ABA needed television, too. So they turned to a television name as their new boss and hired Jack Dolph, who left his job as director of sports for CBS.

As Dolph assumed his new job, Barry and Boone and their partners were selling the Oakland franchise to Earl Foreman, a lawyer from Washington, D.C., who had previously been involved in the ownership of the NFL's Philadelphia Eagles, the NBA's Baltimore Bullets, and the Washington Whips of the North American Soccer League. Well, they weren't exactly selling. The Bank of America was ready to foreclose on a $1.2 million note to the Oaks owners. To protect its investment the bank made a deal with Foreman, awarding him an interest-free note to be paid out of his profits when the team was sold. Foreman was immediately given $500,000 in operating expenses from the league to move the team to Washington, D.C. He was already way ahead of the game.

But Washington, too, was a questionable sports market. The city and its metropolitan area had supported the Redskins, but had failed to support two different versions of baseball's Senators. Of course, not many teams that are losers gain a following. And the Senators were the most notorious losers of all time. It was generally accepted that if they ever won a pennant, it would be a miracle. A successful novel and a hit Broadway play were based on satirizing that miracle. The play *Damn Yankees* ran for more than two years. That was longer than the basketball team would run in Washington.

Basketball appeared to have an open-armed market in Washington. It was a predominantly black city. A ghetto-filled city. It had terrific high school basketball and had yielded such pro stars as Elgin Baylor and Dave

Bing. But there was no suitable place for the team to play in. Washington might have been the only pro-sized city in America without a pro-sized arena. It was natural that an ABA team would end up there.

The Washington Caps, as the team was renamed, played in an old and cold barn called the Washington Coliseum. It held maybe 5,000 people. I had once gone to see Bruno Sammertino wrestle Killer Kowalski there, and I thought the whole place was going to cave in when the two behemoths hit the mat together.

When Barry recovered from early-season injuries, the Caps were able to fill the place up. But even if filled, no team could ever make enough money to survive by playing there.

So Earl Foreman went looking for a pro-size arena. He found two in the planning stages, but both were in Virginia. Norfolk and Hampton Roads. Surely not pro-size cities. But you can't have everything. He couldn't make it in a pro-size city without a pro-size arena, so Foreman tried pro-size arenas in minor-league cities.

Foreman moved his Washington caps to Virginia, where they became known as the Virginia Squires, and set up the league's second "regional" franchise. The first regional franchise had been started the year before when the team from Houston had moved to Carolina. A "regional" franchise is a team that plays its home games in a number of different arenas in a number of different cities. Kind of like Ringling Brothers Barnum and Bailey Circus. Trouble is the circus can decide how many dates to play according to how populated the city is; the regional franchise has to play forty or so home games no matter what. Foreman probably would have been better off back in Oakland.

Right about this time Rick Barry decided he wanted out. Playing in Oakland wasn't so bad, especially with his father-in-law there. But playing in that barn in Washington was a joke. The only thing that might be worse was playing in Norfolk, Virginia. Even Joe Namath wouldn't have been a star playing football in Norfolk. So Barry went and told some Virginia newspapermen that he wanted to get out so his kids wouldn't grow up saying "you all." That was all the people in Virginia had to hear. Foreman had to get rid of him.

Earl sold Barry to the New York Nets. In return he got a reported $250,000. Barry went to New York and discovered that playing in the ABA wasn't so bad after all. Foreman stayed in Virginia and discovered there was a way to get some money out of all this. He was never going to make a profit at the gate. And although Jack Dolph had managed to get the league a national contract with CBS (with teams in markets like Salt Lake City, Denver and Hampton, Virginia) they were never going to make much revenue from television. But Foreman realized he could make a ton of money by selling players, just as he had done with Barry. Good players. So while all the other owners were trying to make a buck by getting the best players and having the best team, Earl Foreman sold his best players and had the worst team.

This was the situation the innocent Julius Erving entered into in September of 1971 with his $500,000 contract and no college degree. It was the third step on his unwitting road to obscurity. Roosevelt. Amherst. Now Virginia. And a league that in four seasons had gained as much attention as Spiro Agnew had as Governor of Maryland.

Julius joined the team for a three-day rookie camp in Richmond. On the first day he was jumping so high that Johnny Kerr, the Squires general manager, approached Al Bianchi, the team's coach, and said, "You better get him out of there. You don't want him to hurt himself." Right then the Squires knew they had something special.

Then the veterans came to camp. The players who

the year before had won 55 games and lost 29 and were the Eastern Division champions and bowed to Kentucky in the second round of the playoffs.

The star of the team had been Charlie Scott, a rookie from the University of North Carolina and Julius' teammate on the Westsiders in the Rucker League. He had played in all 84 of the Squires' games and had finished with a scoring average of 27.10 points a game, fifth best in the league. He made the all-league team and tied for rookie-of-the-year honors with Kentucky's Dan Issel. Scott was a freewheeling guard who loved to shoot and had to have the ball.

Most of his offensive support came from George Carter, a six-foot-five-inch forward who averaged 18.94 points a game. Carter had grown up in Buffalo, New York and had gone to St. Bonaventure College in that area. He had graduated in 1967 and joined the Detroit Pistons of the NBA. But after having played only five minutes of one game the first week of the season, he received his draft notice and was ordered to report to San Francisco. He spent the next two years playing for the all-army team. When he got out in 1969 he joined the Washington Caps and averaged 14.4 points a game.

The Squires all reported to training camp and got their first look at their rookie sensation, Julius Erving. For George Carter it was not a long look. After the first week of camp he was traded to the Pittsburgh Condors for a first-round draft choice. He went from a first-place team with a rookie sensation to the most poorly organized, poorly supported team in the league.

"I knew right from the beginning that Julius was going to play forty minutes a game for us," Bianchi said. "And so both of them couldn't be happy. So I had to get rid of George."

"I was absolutely stunned when Virginia traded me," George says. "It changed my whole perspective on the game. I realized that no matter how much you may contribute to your team, you're still trade bait. They'll get rid of you if they want someone else. I really hated them for trading me. But I decided I had to just forget about all the bullshit and do the job they were paying me for in Pittsburgh. You always like to be idealistic and think that this is more than a job. But it's not."

The 1971 season began for the Squires, and Julius and Charlie Scott quickly proved themselves to be an exciting combination. Charlie was a ball-handling guard who had to control the ball and the game. Julius was the high-jumping forward who would take the offensive rebound, do a little dance under the basket, and put it in. They could both run all night. And so Bianchi installed a wide-open, fast-break, offensive attack.

The fast break has become the dominant style in professional basketball. It is a style that requires constant running. The team counts on two of its five players to get the defensive rebounds, and the three remaining team members run down the court. They try to get there before the opposition has a chance to set up their defense. The object is to race the ball up the court and take the shot before the opponents are ready to guard their men. A successful fast-breaking team depends on a strong rebounder who gets a high percentage of the defensive rebounds, and a few good shooters, who can make a high percentage of their shots. The style was perfected by the old Boston Celtics, who won 11 titles in 13 NBA seasons between 1956 and 1969. Their success depended on the rebounding ability of Bill Russell and the shooting of Bob Cousy, Bill Sharman, and Sam Jones.

Julius added a new dimension to the break. He could get the rebound at the defensive end of the court and race down to the other end just as his teammates were shooting. Then he was in position for the offensive rebound as well. As good as a shooting guard may be— and Charlie Scott is among the best—the basketball crowd is still most excited by the men who operate in, near the basket, where they use their jumping ability along with their shooting ability. It's the athlete who can rise high above the rim, high above the arms of the other nine jumping players, grabbing the ball with his arms outstretched, who draws the real roar from the crowd. This is probably because although the average fan might shoot and dribble to some degree, he can never jump this high off the ground. Julius' arms were above all the others constantly. His high-wire act, Bianchi called it. It was apparent that people were coming to see him and not Charlie Scott.

"We had a definite problem there," Bianchi says. "The fans naturally gravitated from Charlie to Julie. Julius was thrilling on the court and so mature off it. Charlie was just a child.

"To balance Julie's dominance, Charlie wanted to win the league scoring title. I knew it. He knew it. Julie knew it. Julie was mature enough to accept it and to fit his game to that fact.

"Charlie would shoot and shoot. One night he scored 49 points and afterward I told him he played a terrible game."

The Squires were having a good year, but they were trailing the Kentucky Colonels, who were heading for a record number of wins for a season behind their seven-foot rookie center, Artis Gilmore. Scott was heading for that scoring title. And Julius was among the league leaders in both scoring and rebounding.

Around New Year's Julius stepped back for a moment to evaluate his situation with the Squires. He realized what the other rookies who came into the pros were making. He realized that he was being shortchanged.

The $125,000 a year he had been promised was to be paid as a $75,000 salary and $50,000 in deferred payments. But Julius found himself in some financial difficulty and wanted to restructure his contract. The NBA was planning its draft, and Julius was eligible since his class was graduating. He realized that he was in an excellent bargaining position because of his performance in the pros so far. He may not have been a publicly recognized star, but all the pro teams in both leagues recognized his ability.

He went to Bob Woolf and asked him to go in and renegotiate for him. Woolf refused on principal. So Julius' teammate Fatty Taylor introduced him to his agent, Irwin Weiner. Weiner is the brains behind a management firm called Walt Frazier Enterprises, which uses the high-living Knicks star as a front to attract athletes. Weiner flew down to Virginia and met with Julius and they were in business.

Weiner apparently approached Earl Foreman and asked him to renegotiate the contract. Foreman refused. Weiner then asked for the guaranteed deferred money to be paid then. Foreman told him, "My personal guarantee is not worth a pile of dirty jockstraps." That was all Weiner had to hear.

He felt the Squires were reneging on their obligation. And so he went looking for a better deal for his client. As he approached NBA teams, he explained that Julius had three more years on his contract with Virginia, but he showed them that contract and explained that he was going to try to have it rescinded. He explained to the interested parties that there were three alternatives: The contract could be tested in court to see if Foreman had violated his obligation; it could be bought from the Squires; or Julius could be signed to a contract that would begin three years after this one expired.

Weiner found a taker in Bill Putnam, the president of the Atlanta Hawks of the NBA. Putnam knew all about the dirty fighting that went on in the basketball war. He had lost two players, Zelmo Beatty, his center, and Joe Caldwell, a forward, to the upstart league. He was more than willing to get back at them. The league's college

draft, the designated procedure by which to acquire
players, was still a few months away, but Putnam did
not think it necessary for him to wait. "I viewed this as
the same situation as when the Supersonics signed Spencer Haywood," Putnam said. "He had signed a contract
before his class graduated and so he was elegible for
our draft. He was already a pro."

So Putnam signed Julius to a five-year contract that
was reported to include a $250,000 bonus on the spot, a
$250-a-month apartment in Atlanta and a new $9,000
blue Jaguar. The salary was $200,000 for the first year,
rising to $215,000, $230,000, $245,000 and $260,000 each
year, with $75,000 paid up front by October 1 of each
year. There were also seven clauses stricken from or
amended in the regular player's contract. One gave
Julius the right to name four teams to which he could
refuse to be traded. The other forbade the team from
telling him how to dress or act in public. The playoffs
were near and Julius did not want to upset his team, so
the parties agreed not to announce the contract until the
season was over. Julius returned to play for the Squires.

Had Charlie Scott known what had happened, his
whole life might have been different. But he was upset
with the way the Virginia fans had embraced Julius and
he wanted out. After 73 games of the 84-game season
Scott had established a new league record of 2,524 points
for a season and had assured himself of the league scoring championship. The next night he left the Squires. He
showed up a few days later in the uniform of the
Phoenix Suns of the NBA.

"Charlie was down on himself," Bianchi said. "He
thought we didn't appreciate him, but the NBA was
offering him a lot of money, so they did. So he split."

The NBA draft was scheduled for April. On April 9
word got out that Julius was jumping to the Hawks. The
report then was that Putnam saw he was in a position to
get some revenge and hurt the other league, so he an-

nounced the move. He claims, however, that the leak came from the Carolinas. He doesn't know where. Just from the Carolinas. He had ignored a dictum by NBA Commissioner Walter Kennedy that the league honor all existing ABA contract and had also circumvented the next day's official draft.

On April 10 the Milwaukee Bucks, ignoring the report from Atlanta, went ahead and drafted Julius in the first round. They had two first-round selections, having obtained one in a trade with the Houston Rockets. "You have to assume that with two first-round picks you are not going to sign both of them," says Wayne Embry, the general manager of the Bucks. "You can't afford to. So I figured, why not own the rights to the best player in the ABA. You never know what's going to happen over there.

"Atlanta had acted with complete disrespect for the rule governing our league. I figured there was no way for them to get away with what they did."

So as the Squires prepared for the second round of the playoffs against the Nets, they thought Julius was on their team. The Atlanta Hawks had a signed contract that said he was joining their team. And the Milwaukee Bucks had the draft rights that required him to play for their team. It all sounded like a skit that Groucho Marx dreamed up.

On April 13 the semifinal playoff series began. Julius played as well as ever, but the Nets, led by former Squire Rick Barry, won in 6 games. The season was over for the Squires. And none of them really expected Julius to be back the next year.

"That Weiner has disrupted my team," Bianchi said. "If I get hold of him, I'm going to put his nose where his ear is."

After the season Julius moved into the apartment the Hawks had provided for him in Atlanta. Weiner had instructed him to go there so the Squires could not sub-poena him and prevent him from leaving the state.

"Julius really liked Atlanta," Dave Brownbill says. "It has a lot of black people. It seemed like a progressive city. He felt like the city was on the move.

"He was really looking forward to playing there. Julius is the kind of person who prepares himself for the kinds of things he is going to do."

While living in Atlanta, Julius would commute to New York on weekends to play for the Westsiders in the Rucker League. He worked on his game, anticipating the competition in the NBA. After Brownbill closed the park where he worked for the night, he and Julius would turn on the lights and work out. Julius felt that the tall centers in the NBA would cut off a lot of his lanes to the basket. So from midnight until five A.M. they would work on his outside shooting.

Like most athletes, Julius was often approached by people who needed something from him. He liked to help out whenever he could. But a good number of the people were only looking to take advantage of him.

"This guy named Milt came up to me at one game," Brownbill says, "and said he was running a game at Benjamin Franklin High School in the city for the benefit of Harlem Prep. So I got him Julius and Nate Archibald and Dave Stallworth for a tiny guarantee.

"My girlfriend, Franny, was collecting the money. During halftime they had a hot pants contest, and while it was going on, Milt switched the cash boxes on Franny and took off. We never saw him again. We didn't even have enough money to give the girl with the best legs the twenty-five dollars she won.

"And then there's a guy we'll call Alabama. He is notorious for starting tournaments, taking the money, and skipping town.

"One day he ran a game at Brandeis High School and I got Julius to play for him. He wrote bad checks to everyone, even to the cab driver who took him to the game. The meter read $2.50 and Alabama told the driver he had no cash but would write him a check for $5. The cabbie took it. Alabama ran. The check bounced as high as Julius jumps."

But while Julius was spending the summer on the court, other people were in the court deciding where he would spend his winter.

On June 14, Louis Nizer, the attorney for Walt Frazier Enterprises, filed a suit in Eastern District Court to "rescind, vacate and terminate" the contract to the Squires. The suit claimed that Steve Arnold, the agent who first contacted Julius with the offer from the ABA, was representing both the player and the league at the same time. "Arnold, at the time he represented or purported to represent the plaintiff [Erving] in negotiation of the aforesaid agreement, acted on behalf and in the interest of the defendant [Squires] and the ABA had failed diligently to exploit more favorable opportunities for the plaintiff, and Arnold received compensation from the defendant for services rendered to it or on its behalf therefore."

Erving also sued for damages in the amount of $308,000 with interest. The contract was for four years, and Foreman was supposed to have given written agreement of a personal guarantee he had made to assure Julius of compensation if the team or the league folded. Foreman had done no such thing.

A city marshal was looking for Foreman to serve a subpoena but could not find him. "A subpoena from Weiner. Sounds great, doesn't it?" Johnny Kerr said when he heard about it.

When training camp started in September, Julius was in Atlanta with the Hawks. He enjoyed being with the Hawks. He liked Cotton Fitzsimmons, the coach. And he even enjoyed playing on a team with Pete Maravich.

No one expected the two of them to be able to play together. Maravich had the most moves of any guard in the game. And Julius had the most moves of any forward. It was like Fred Astaire and Gene Kelly dancing together.

Julius played in two exhibition games with the Hawks. And on one particular play the two flashy stars reached an understanding. The Hawks cleared a rebound and Maravich and Erving ran down the floor on a two-on-one fast break. Maravich took the outlet pass, put the ball through his legs, the defensive man came up on him, and he whipped a pass behind his back to Julius. Then Julius put the ball through his legs, the man moved over, and he whipped it behind his back to Maravich. But Pete was so surprised to have the ball back that he walked.

He looked at Julius. He was embarrassed. He smiled and said, "Okay, Doc." That was all. They were set after that.

In one of those games, against the Carolina Cougars in Raleigh, North Carolina, Julius scored 32 points, hitting on 14 of 15 shots, and had 10 rebounds. As he walked off the court at game's end, a small boy asked him for one of the white sweatbands on his wrist. Julius took it off and gave it to the boy, a gesture most athletes wouldn't even think of.

Before Julius had left Virginia at the end of the previous season, he had arranged with Al Bianchi for Dave Brownbill to get an invitation to the Squires rookie camp. So while Julius was in Atlanta, Brownbill was in Virginia. Under the circumstances he was in the wrong place at the wrong time.

"Al Bianchi came up to me as soon as I arrived there," Brownbill says, "and told me honestly that even if I played good ball for three weeks, I didn't have a chance of making the team." The Squires had signed three rookie guards, Mike Barr, Dave Twardzik, and Billy Shepherd, to no-cut contracts, and they were obligated to pay them whether they kept them or not.

"I told all this to Julius," Brownbill says, "and he felt bad. But what could he do? He wanted to stay in Atlanta.

"The players on the Squires would come up to me and ask about Julius. I was caught in the middle. I thought he was my way to the top. Instead I was hurt by association.

"One of the players, George Irvine, came up to me and said, 'I sure hope Julius comes back. My career depends on it. I need his strength for me to make this team. My talent won't fit in too many other places.'"

Just before the teams went to camp the ABA owners decided to replace Commissioner Jack Dolph. He had negotiated a national television contract, as he had promised. But it had not provided nearly as much revenue for each team as the owners had expected.

During Dolph's tenure the league had managed to put the players' salary structure at a peak that owners in neither league could handle and had forced the NBA to agree to seek congressional approval of a merger. So as its new boss, the owners turned to corporate lawyer Bob Carlson. "Don't even give me a contract," Carlson said. "All I want to do is get a merger."

On September 13, with all the teams in both leagues in training camps, Carlson filed a suit in criminal court to prevent Erving from playing with any team but the Squires.

On September 23, Julius defied an NBA Board of Governors ruling that said he was the property of the Milwaukee Bucks and played in an exhibition game for the Atlanta Hawks. At the same time Julius and the Atlanta Hawks filed a $2 million suit against the NBA claiming that the common draft is a violation of the Sherman

Antitrust Act. By so doing they were really involving themselves in brinkmanship, figuring the NBA did not want to take a chance in court and possibly have their draft ruled illegal. Putnam, too, would be distressed if he did end up in court and won his own case.

On September 26 Commissioner Walter Kennedy fined the Hawks $25,000 for using Erving in two exhibition games.

On October 2 Judge E. R. Neaher offered an injunction in New York that barred Julius from playing with anyone but the Squires. He ordered the Squires to settle the contract by arbitration. And so Julius returned home to New York to await the settlement or even sit out the year if he had to. Carlson immediately appointed Donald Dell, an attorney and former captain of the U.S. Davis Cup team, as the arbitrator. Later in the year Dell removed himself from the case and was replaced by a Harvard Law School professor named Archibald Cox, who would later become famous as the special prosecutor in the Watergate affair.

On October 19 Erving announced that he would rejoin the Squires pending disposition of the court suit to break his four-year contract with the Squires.

On October 24 a three-judge panel headed by Judge H. R. Medina, in answer to an appeal of the injunction prohibiting Erving from playing anywhere but in Virginia, affirmed that decision until an arbitrator was named in the contract dispute.

Without Julius, the Squires had lost their first 4 games of the 1972 season. He returned to the team in New York on October 20, scored 26 points, pulled down 11 rebounds, and the Squires won their first game of the year over the Nets 130–120.

The next night they returned home to Norfolk to face the Cougars at Scope. Julius had tried to turn his back on the team and had to be told by a court to return. And yet on that night 9,185 fans, almost twice as many as the team would average for the season, turned out to welcome him back and gave him a standing ovation when he was introduced.

"He is the kind of guy who never closes doors behind him," Bianchi says. "Charlie Scott could never have returned and been accepted. But no matter where Julius might go, they would always love him here."

Julius scored 23 points, had 16 rebounds, and the Squires won again, 119–110. They won in Memphis and then back home against Denver, 155–111, in a game in which Denver coach Alex Hannum told his players to foul intentionally as a criticism of the competence of the ABA refs.

Julius Erving is proud. Too proud to let legal battles affect his play.

The court could be in Virginia or Atlanta or rough asphalt in Harlem. He will always do whatever is necessary to convince everyone looking on that he is the best one out there. In his lame-duck year in Virginia he did the same thing he did when those rough kids wanted to fight him in the playgrounds. He put the ball to the floor, went to the hoop, and showed them who was boss.

After 4 games the Squires were 0 and 4. After 8 games, with Julius back, they were 4 and 4. But they were a mediocre team, and it was only because of his presence that they were able to finish the season at .500. Julius won his first league scoring championship in 1972–1973. He averaged 31.94 points per game. With 22 points he was the leading scorer in the All-Star game in Salt Lake City. And he was voted to the all-league team. The Squires were eliminated in the first round of the playoffs by the Kentucky Colonels, 4 games to 1. But Julius had had his own best season ever. He knew in the beginning of the season that he had to. He had to show that he was above all the off-court bickering. He wanted to be treated fairly, but whatever the situation, his first love was basketball.

The season ended and the speculation began again. Virginia still had two more years on their contract. And Putnam and Embry were continuing to meet to reach some kind of settlement between them, a trade or a pay-off that would leave Julius in Atlanta and Milwaukee satisfied.

But two situations developed that would turn the whole ongoing battle around.

In Atlanta neither the Hawks nor the NHL Flames, the two teams owned by the Omni Corporation, were showing any signs of heading toward a profit, and much of the blame was placed on Putnam's tactics. The nine stockholders, led by John Wilcox, wanted to push Putnam out, and they used the Julius Erving case as the basis. They could not understand Putnam's paying money up front for a player of any caliber. Putnam had felt he made an excellent investment in the future no matter what the immediate decisions yielded. But he was forced out. And Wilcox became president promising to look for some way out of the controversial and costly situation.

Meanwhile Earl Foreman was facing a loss of $700,000 during the season with the Squires. On top of that he had incurred $200,000 in legal fees fighting for Julius. He no longer had the money to stay in the game. As he had with Barry, he decided the way to save himself was to get rid of his best player. By doing so he would rid himself of the legal expenses, keep Erving in his own league, and get Atlanta off his back. He would also rid himself of the only attractive aspect of his franchise, but that was the chance he had to take.

Roy Boe had decided he needed a major attraction. He had had it in Rick Barry and had lost him to the NBA. He tried to have it with Jim Chones, but had made a mistake. Now he could get the most exciting ballplayer in the league, a local Long Island boy.

And so on July 31 the caper was pulled off.

Atlanta was paid $1,000,000, a considerable profit above the $259,000 they had already laid out for Julius. And Wilcox kept his promise to his partners.

Virginia was paid $1,000,000, relieved of the burden of Julius' contract, and given George Carter, who had been so incensed when the Squires traded him away three years earlier. The Nets included in the deal the rights to Kermit Washington, a graduating senior from American University.

Milwaukee was given nothing. The Bucks had apparently offered to make the same kind of settlement that Boe was attempting to make in his league. They felt the Virginia contract was invalid, as Weiner had told them, but they were willing to take advantage of Wilcox's coup and pay off Atlanta.

"Embry was in my office last week," Weiner said. "He said they would come up with a package and would work it out with Atlanta. They never got back to us and never offered us one single dollar."

Julius came home to Roosevelt again for the summer of 1973, just as he had done each of the five summers since he had gone away to school. But this time it was different. When the summer ended, he wasn't going anyplace. He was home for good.

Julius might have been richer than ever, but he was just as susceptible to basketball parasites. Despite his reputation as a thief, Alabama dared to show up again in New York that summer. He contacted Dave Brownbill and told him he was running an all-star basketball benefit in New Jersey. He said he had already enlisted Mo Layton of the Phoenix Suns and Harthorne Wingo of the Knicks and he wanted Brownbill and Julius. He said he would pay Julius $3,000 and Brownbill $125. Julius didn't really need the cash now, but he went along because Brownbill did.

At half time Alabama came into the locker room with

a long look on his face. He told Julius that he had expected a sellout but he had been wrong. Julius knew what was coming, so he demanded his money. Alabama handed him $1,000 and Julius headed back to the court for the second half. But Alabama was sitting in the locker room with his head in his hands, talking to himself, asking how he was going to pay everyone else now that he had given Julius $1,000. Julius came back, handed him $500 and played the second half. He finished the game with 50 points.

A few weeks later Alabama called Brownbill again. He told him he wanted to buy him lunch. Brownbill met him at the agreed-upon restaurant, but he left his own wallet home. That was the only way he could be sure Alabama would pay.

"He sat down and pulled out this notebook and showed me this whole tour he had mapped out," Brownbill says. "He would take a team to Curaçao, Surinam, Mexico, and Trinidad and showed me written guarantees in each place that amounted to $140,000. He said he was going to pay the players $600 a week and he wanted me to line them up.

"Of course, there was one slight problem already. Alabama needed some expense money to get started. About $2,000. He read about how much Julius was making, and he figured he could afford to put it up."

Julius brought the copies of the guarantees to Irwin Weiner, and Weiner lent Alabama the $2,000. Then Alabama disappeared for two months.

Then one day Alabama called Brownbill from Venezuela and told him to buy the uniforms and get ready to leave. He was sending him plane tickets. Brownbill bought the uniforms. He still has them.

"A week later Julius got a call from Alabama asking him for money to bail him out of the clink," Brownbill says. "Julius hung up on him and we both kissed the whole thing good-bye.

"I don't know how he did it, but Alabama finally did get a team of twenty-five guys down there. They went to Aruba first. The plane tickets cost $49,000 and they ran up a bar bill of $4,000 the first week. They played eleven games, but no one got paid."

Finally three of the players took Alabama into an alley and broke his jaw and three of his ribs. "They were doing the job for all of us," Brownbill says.

Then they paid their own way home.

No one heard from him for another six months. But at the beginning of the new pro season he called Tommy Taylor, Julius' former high school teammate and at that time a player in the Eastern League. He told Taylor he was taking a team to Brazil. Taylor hung up on him.

Brownbill expects that someone is going to hear from Alabama again soon. He keeps coming back. Like a rash.

6. Getting Out of One Mess . . .

The 1974 ABA All-Star game was played at Scope, that pro-size arena that had attracted Earl Foreman to Norfolk, Virginia. So I took the opportunity to go there and see what Julius had left behind.

Right from the beginning of the new season, Foreman had been up to his old, money-making tricks. He was still trading away good players to keep his head temporarily above water rather than trying to build a good team and a successful franchise.

He had used one of two first-round picks in 1973 to get Swen Nater, a six-foot-eleven athlete who had played back-up center to Bill Walton, the college player of the year for two years, while they were both at UCLA. Nater got his chance to play as a pro and averaged 14 points and 10 rebounds a game early in the season for the Squires. But once again Foreman found himself in need of cash, and he sold Nater to the San Antonio Spurs for a reported $400,000. He would help that team finish second in their division and by season's end become the league's best home draw. They would average close to 10,000 fans a game through the last month of the season. And Nater would be voted the ABA's rookie of the year.

I arrived in Norfolk on the morning of the All-Star game. I got into a cab at the airport, and as I rode through the side streets of the city, I was startled at how similar it looked to Roosevelt, Long Island. Both the occupied and unoccupied store-fronts looked uncared for.

The main difference between the Southern city and Northern suburb was a two-block stretch that interrupted the atmosphere.

On these neatly landscaped, shining white, brick blocks Scope was located. Not *the* Scope. Just Scope. And across the street was the fourteen-story Holiday Inn where the players and the press were staying. The writers were all running around in different directions trying to find Foreman. The rumor was that he had done it again. He had sold his best player and only legitimate All-Star, George Gervin, to San Antonio for a reported $300,000. Commissioner Mike Storen was shocked. Gervin was the last player of star quality that the Squires had left. If he was sold the team was as faceless as a tennis racket. Storen told a gathering of press that if any such deal had indeed been made, he would veto it.

Finally Foreman did appear in the press suite.

"Did you really do it?" Butch van Breda Kolff, the coach of the Memphis Tams, asked.

There was no answer.

One by one the writers approached Foreman for an answer.

"No comment," he said again and again.

While I was waiting around for the game to begin, I did run into George Carter, the man who had been traded away from two different teams to make room for Julius. I had not seen George all season, but I followed his statistics. He was the Squires' second leading scorer behind Gervin.

He was averaging close to 20 points a game as he had done once before in Virginia and also in Pittsburgh, in Carolina, and in New York. He was bought from Carolina by the Nets in 1973 to replace Rick Barry as their shooting forward after Rick was forced to go back to the NBA. In his year there he had been the team's leading scorer. George was a shooter. He would score well on every team he played with. The way his career was going, he might get the chance to score for every team. He was good enough so that any team could use him. But not so good that they could not get rid of him if something better were offered.

Trading is a procedure that is peculiar to sports. Factories do not trade workers and schools do not trade teachers. But the supply of athletic talent is limited and teams use their players as bait to obtain what they hope are better players. The trade causes ambivalent feelings among both players and fans. A player on a losing team can enjoy the fact if he is traded to a better team. Or a player who is sitting on the bench can enjoy being sent to a team he will play for. On the other hand, a deal can work the opposite way. And no matter what the result, the traded player always has to face the problems of uprooting himself and his family and settling in a new environment.

The fan enjoys seeing a good player come to his team, but resents seeing his favorite player go elsewhere. But the fans' memories are usually much shorter than those of the players experiencing the deal. In most cases they root for the team whoever the players are. And soon they will take to the new team members.

Carter had been traded from good situations to bad situations and from bad situations to good. But coming to Virginia, where he had once been rejected, to a team that was ridding itself of the best player in the league had to be the worst situation he ever faced.

We went into the bar and ordered a beer and began talking. He obviously had a lot on his mind and he was glad there was someone to listen.

"The Nets were a young team last year and we had a lot of problems," he said. "And Lou Carnesecca [the coach] didn't help solve any of them. He pounded things in and made them worse.

"At the end of the year we all knew there would be

a shakeup, but we didn't know who would go. Louie was the first to leave and that was a good sign.

"I felt I had had a pretty good year for them and I wondered who they could possibly trade me for. But when you have a chance to get Julius, you trade five players if you have to. Roy Boe is competing with the Knicks in that town and he needs the players who can draw. He would have given up his whole team for Julius.

"I was in Pittsburgh for the summer and Irwin Weiner called me to tell me what had transpired." Suddenly I remembered that Weiner was Carter's agent, too. He had arranged a deal for one of his clients at the expense of another.

"He told me what was happening," George continued, "and I was really pissed off. I said that I had played well for Virginia once already and they didn't want me then. Why would they want me now?

"I really felt animosity toward this team when they traded me the first time. I was stunned. I hated them for it. So I hated to come back and play for them again.

"My first reaction was that I am a tool and they are all just using me. But, shit, I'm using them, too. I'm getting paid. So I just go out and do my job. I don't talk to nobody here now. I just do my job."

I asked him if it's flattering to be traded for a player the calibre of Julius, and that offended him.

"I'm not flattered. I don't think Julius will be any better for that club than I was. I was pissed off.

"But I adjusted. I said to myself that a lot of guys wouldn't have been able to adjust. They would have lost the concept of their job. But I'm scoring here just like I did every place else.

"My son's only two years old now, so the moving around isn't all that bad. If he was in school, it would be different. But I love the game and I love the money.

"You just got to remember that there's no support in this game. The only support you get is from yourself.

It's easy to get down on yourself. I've done that in the past. But no more. I've learned. I'm a veteran of the basketball war."

That night the All-Star game was played before a capacity crowd at Scope, the largest crowd ever to see a sporting event in Virginia. Anyone who had attended a Squires game all year must have shown up there that night.

The Squires had two representatives on the East team, George Gervin and Jim Eakins, who was selected after the Nets' Billy Paultz had to withdraw because of an injury. Before the game the players were all introduced and there was obligatory clapping. No official announcement of the rumored transaction was made, and Gervin was introduced as a representative of the Squires. He got some more emotional applause. So did Eakins. But the crowd saved themselves for Julius. They welcomed him just as they had the night he had returned from Atlanta—with a standing ovation.

As it turned out, the star of the game was former Squire Swen Nater. He scored 29 points and pulled down a game record 22 rebounds. A sign in the crowd painted on black paper pictured a man with a rope around his neck and read, "Sell Foreman." It best expressed the sentiments of the crowd. Nater's performance encouraged those feelings.

But the play of the night was pulled off by Julius. He had sat back most of the game and let the other All-Stars perform. But at a point early in the second half Ted McClain of Carolina stole the ball and lofted a long pass over everyone into the out-stretched arms of the Doctor. He was all alone and could shoot anyway he desired. You could feel the crowd holding its breath, waiting to explode. He dribbled underneath the basket and dunked the ball back over his head and through the hoop. The building exploded into a sonorous roar as if Arnold Palmer had made a tournament-winning putt on the eighteenth green. Eleven thousand people slapped five with whoever was sitting next to them.

After the game the league had a party at the Holiday Inn. Earl Foreman had told me to meet him there to talk. He was nowhere to be found. And I knew I didn't have to wait around.

The next morning I went back to Scope, where the Squires were scheduled to practice, to meet with Al Bianchi.

Bianchi had been a hard-nosed guard for ten years with the Syracuse Nationals of the NBA, and when they moved, with the Philadelphia Seventy-Sixers. He averaged 8 points a game over that career. His outstanding quality was his toughness. He would push people around. In pro basketball pushing people around is an important talent that goes unnoticed by the average fan. If a defensive player leans on his man, bumps into him, and hand checks him for the first half, by the critical closing minutes of the game that man is worn down physically and unable to run as hard and jump as high as he might have earlier. Al Bianchi liked to lean on people. The only category he ever led the league in was most games disqualified from on fouls in a season. He did that twice.

Bianchi was hired away from the NBA's Seattle Supersonics when Foreman moved his team to Washington, D.C. In Bianchi's first five years, Foreman sold Rick Barry, Swen Nater, George Gervin, and Julius Erving, lost Charlie Scott to the NBA, and let signed contracts with Dave Bing and Bob McAdoo dissolve so that they both ended up in the other league. If he had them all, he would have had the best team in the history of the game.

How can a man have all this happen around him and still stay on as a coach?

"I'm just not sure," he says, "that even with everything that has happened here, I could ever duplicate my coach-owner relationship anyplace else. I have security here. Security is the key to my job.

"It used to be that a coach would have to worry about waking up each morning and making sure he still has his job. But now you wake up and run for the morning papers to see which superstar you've lost today."

The day before, while all the rumors about the Gervin deal were circulating around the hotel, the reporters looked for Bianchi. When they found him, all he could say was he didn't know any more than they did. "The only thing that is upsetting me," he said cunningly, "is that while I'm staying here to talk to you reporters I'm missing my tennis game."

Bianchi put on a sweat shirt and gym shorts and walked out onto the empty Scope floor to meet his team for practice. The eleven o'clock news the night before and the morning Virginia newspapers had announced that Gervin had been traded. But still no official announcement had been made. Bianchi swore he still had heard nothing about any such deal.

Gervin, a six-foot-nine-inch forward who is as thin as the stick in an ice-cream pop, was on the court going two-on-two with some teammates.

"Hey, G.G.," Bianchi said, "you hear all those things they're saying about you? You're not going anywhere. No, sir."

Bianchi sat on a folding chair alongside the court as his players ran wildly up and down the floor in what was called practice, but was more like a schoolyard pickup game.

"If I worried about all these kinds of things, I'd have an ulcer, right?" he said, looking at me as if I had to agree with him. "I taught myself a long time ago in this game you can't worry about the things which you can do nothing about. Like I told you yesterday, the only thing I'm upset about is that I missed my tennis game."

He swung the whistle chain back and forth as if it were his tennis racket. He had to try to thing about something other than this team.

The faceless players, a mixture of small rookies and second-year men and big men he had picked up after they had failed to impress coaches elsewhere, ran up and down having a good time. He stood and watched them as I asked him about Julius. It seemed like a cruel thing to bring up at this time, but he rather enjoyed talking about him.

"When he came here for the playoffs after the contract with Atlanta was announced, I sat down with him like I always had. You can talk to Julius.

"I didn't know if anything had been reneged on in his contract like his agent, Irwin Weiner, said. Weiner had obviously rationalized for him that he hadn't done anything wrong. He told him he was just signing a deal with Atlanta for when his deal with Virginia was over.

"I told him that he had to realize that he was holding the fate of a lot of people in his hands. I said he could strike a death blow to this franchise and to the league if he left. I said, 'You're gonna be well off. You're always gonna be well off. But there will be a lot of other guys out of work.'

"He just sat there and let it sink in and nodded his head. That's what he always does. He says, 'I understand what you're saying,' and you believe him. Then you hope he makes the decision you want.

"I told him just to do what he thought was right and I would have no personal animosity towards him.

"I had a relationship with the kid and a separate relationship with the agent. I wasn't going to confuse the two."

Julius had decided to go to Atlanta, but a judge decided he had to come back to Virginia. So Bianchi had him on his team for one more year. "I still like Julius,"

Bianchi said. "And I still look forward to seeing him play. Too bad it's against us."

He took the whistle from around his neck and ran out onto the floor to scrimmage with his players. And I left Scope to catch a plane back to New York. I had not spoken to Earl Foreman. But I knew there was no chance I was going to. He was in hiding. And I couldn't blame him.

The next day I came into the office of *Sport* magazine and told one of the editors about how the reporters had created the Gervin trade story at the All-Star game. I said it was good copy since such games are dull and provide nothing exciting to write about. "But of course it isn't true," I said. "I was standing right there when Al Bianchi told Gervin that it wasn't true."

That night San Antonio was visiting the Nets at the Nassau Coliseum. I had been so impressed with Swen Nater at the All-Star game than I went out there to see him again.

I sat down at the press table at courtside, right next to the guy who was doing the radio broadcast back to San Antonio. At the half he was handed an announcement to read by Spurs' general manager, Jack Ankerson. It said that the Spurs were filing suit against the Virginia Squires for George Gervin. Half the deal had indeed been made. The Spurs had already given the money to Foreman, but Foreman had not sent the player in return.

Commissioner Mike Storen tried again to overrule the trade, but a court ruled that the deal was final and Gervin was the property of the Spurs.

I still can't forget that scene in Scope. Bianchi telling Gervin, "Hey, G.G., you hear all those stories? You're not going anywhere."

I don't think Bianchi lied to me. And I don't think he lied to Gervin. I think the one thing that keeps Bianchi going while he loses players and games is his relationship with his players. If he lost that, he would have nothing. He couldn't take a chance and tell them a lie. Especially that big a lie.

Until San Antonio filed suit, I don't think Bianchi knew anything about the deal. Earl Foreman had never told him. After all the other ridiculous deals he had made, he must have been afraid to.

The Squires team would have been better if Julius had stayed there. But the organization would not have been. Whether or not he was being ruthless when he asked Weiner to seek a better deal for himself, he was better off out of Virginia. Foreman would spend the rest of the year running the team on a shoestring as he tried to sell it. Under those circumstances even Julius Erving could not help the team.

7. . . . And into Another

So the caper was completed, leaving Julius Erving in New York. Well, not exactly in New York. When you say "New York" in the context of sports, it usually means New York City. In fact, when businessmen who are interested in sports get together to begin a new league, the only rule for them to follow is to put a franchise in New York. To attract attention from the media and a contract from television you must have a team in the city.

The American Basketball Association began by breaking the only rule. Their New York franchise was in New Jersey. Teaneck, New Jersey.

True, New Jersey is close to New York. But only geographically. People from New Jersey come to New York all the time for entertainment. People from New York go to New Jersey only to visit relatives. Having a New York franchise in New Jersey is like having a ski lodge in Miami Beach.

The league did originally intend to have a franchise in New York City. They had awarded it to a man named Arthur Brown, who had come from Chicago and made himself a millionaire in New York in the freight business. Brown was a sports enthusiast who was not satisfied simply buying tickets to see athletes play. He wanted to buy his own athletes. So he hired some to work in his freight business during their offseasons. Mostly he hired players from baseball's New York Mets —Alvin Jackson and Jack Fisher and Bud Harrelson.

81

To run this program he had also hired an athlete, Max Zaslofsky. Max was one of the first stars of professional basketball. He was the leading scorer for the NBA's first western division champion, the Chicago Stags, in 1947, for whom he averaged 14.4 points per game. The next season he won the league scoring title averaging 21 points per game. In 1967 Max's involvement in sports was limited to coaching Brown's company team, which was fittingly named the New York Freighters. Now the ABA was depending on Brown to get them established in New York and Brown was depending on Zaslofsky to get him established in the league.

Brown originally intended his team to play in the Sixty-ninth Regiment Armory on Twenty-third Street in Manhattan, where the NBA's New York entry, the Knicks, had begun their history. But the deal fell through and he was left without a place to play.

As his director of public relations, Brown had hired a man named Murray Goodman. Goodman lived in New Jersey and when the New York City deal fell through, he guided Brown to a neighborhood landmark, the Teaneck Armory, a suburban facility that seated 4,800 people. It was too small a facility to house a successful professional sports franchise. But it was too big for the team Brown named the New Jersey Americans.

The team sold twenty-four season tickets for their first year, sixteen of them to business associates of Arthur Brown. The team could just as well have played in a local movie theater. "If we drew 726, it was a big crowd," says Barney Kremenko, who was hired to assist Goodman and is now still the Nets' PR man.

Brown had assigned one of his most trusted controllers from his freight business to watch over the team for him. The man was an absolute loyalist. Whatever Brown said, or—the controller did.

One of the boss' first instructions was always to be honest when announcing the attendance figures. Brown felt the team would start slowly and build. He thought the local fans would be impressed when they noticed the increase in attendance figures listed in the newspapers. Brown instructed his controller never to announce a crowd of more than 2,000.

Brown was very involved with the team from the beginning. But by Thanksgiving he was already run down by the whole experience, and he decided to take his family away for the weekend so that he could relax.

That Friday night the team held a ceremony honoring a player named Bob Verga, who had grown up in New Jersey. For no apparent reason, on that one Friday night, everyone in New Jersey decided to come see the Americans. When the fire department ruled the doors closed, there were 5,200 people inside and hundreds more who were turned away outside. But Arthur Brown had left his controller with instructions to announce a crowd of no more than 2,000. And that's just what he did.

The Americans were as inconsistent on the court as they were at the box office. They tied the Kentucky Colonels for last place in their division with a record of 36 wins and 42 losses. So the two clubs were forced to play one game to decide who would get the last playoff berth. The Americans were blessed with the honor of having the game on their own home court on the basis of having won the season series from the Colonels, 7 games to 4.

Unfortunately the Teaneck Armory was not expecting the Americans and had made previous plans for that night. So Arthur Brown went looking for a suitable alternative and found one in the Long Island Arena in Commack. The two sites were equally unappealing.

The Teaneck Armory did have a new playing floor, and an offer was made to ship it to Commack for the game. But the officials there said they had their own and it wouldn't be necessary.

On the night of the game the Nets and the Colonels arrived along with a good-sized crowd. But the floor was full of holes wide enough to catch an ankle in. The Colonels refused to play. And Ed Mikan, the brother of Commissioner George Mikan and his assistant, ruled the game a forfeit to Kentucky. The Colonels went to the playoffs and the Americans went home.

But Arthur Brown had not had enough punishment, and he decided to lease the Long Island Arena for the next year. He brought his own floor.

He had heard there were plans for a new Coliseum for Nassau County, and he wanted to be there with a team to occupy it when it was ready. So the New Jersey Americans moved across the state line. They were even farther from New York City than when they were in New Jersey, but they were in the state and thus able to call themselves New York. New York Nets. Just like New York Mets. And New York Jets.

The Arena was a wide-open refrigerator. People would sit in the stands covered with blankets as if they were at a football game. Not many people, though. The only time they drew a decent-sized crowd was the night the Oakland Oaks with Rick Barry came in. But Barry broke his ankle in that game and was out for the rest of the season.

That was only one of many bad breaks for the Nets. In that season they set a league record that still stands for fewest wins in a season—17. By then Brown was completely disgusted with the team and with Zaslofsky. He made one more desperate gesture. He obtained the league's drafts rights to Lew Alcindor, the seven-foot-plus UCLA star. Alcindor, though, did not want to get involved in a long bargaining process. He asked the Nets and the Milwaukee Bucks, who had the draft rights to him in the NBA, each to submit one sealed bid. He would go to the highest bidder. He was all set to go to New York and fully expected them to come up with the cash. But Brown guessed wrong, and Alcindor kept his promise and joined the Bucks.

That was the end. In May of 1969 Brown sold his team to Roy Boe, a Connecticut millionaire who had made his money in a line of women's clothes called Bo-Jest. He paid $988,000 for the team. "All Boe was buying were about five leftover player contracts, a warped basketball floor, some dirty jocks, and a piece of paper that said 'franchise,'" said Bob Carlson, Boe's lawyer. But Boe insisted that Long Island was the fourth-best sports market in the country and he was going to be a success.

His first move toward this end was hiring Lou Carnesecca, the successful coach at St. Johns University, as his coach and general manager. But Carnesecca had a year left on his college contract, which he wanted to complete, so Boe hired York Larese as interim coach.

The team moved into Nassau County, the more populated of the two Long Island counties, and into the Island Garden, which was a more suitable facility. Which is like saying that Agnew is better than Nixon. They finished fourth in their division in 1970–71, with a record of 39 wins and 45 losses, and they took a strong Kentucky club to the seventh game of the playoffs before bowing. The Nets home games were scheduled for Thursday and Sunday in that series. It rained on Friday and the roof of the Island Garden leaked. *Newsday,* the Long Island newspaper, showed a photo of a maintenance man mopping up the place. Boe was upset by the bad publicity. But on Sunday they sold out for the first time. Which confirms the fact that a good leak will attract attention.

The Nets anticipated the beginning of the next season. Lou Carnesecca was coming over. And in September the startling announcement was made that he would be joined by Rick Barry, the best player in the league. Earl Foreman had sold Barry to the Nets for $250,000.

In order to make it against the other seven sports
teams in town Boe needed a name player. One who was
not only good on the court but also on talk shows and
in golf tournaments where the other sports celebrities
appeared. Barry was all these things. Unfortunately he
was also injury prone. He missed much of his first season as a Net. The team was vastly improved, however,
finishing with 40 wins and 44 losses before bowing to
the Charlie Scott version of the Squires in six games in
the playoffs. Billy Paultz, a six-foot-ten-inch center who
had played for Carnesecca at St. Johns, joined the team
that year as did Billy Melchionni, a level headed guard
from the NBA. Together they formed the nucleus to
build a team around.

In the 1971–72 season they got off to a slow start
again. But at mid-season they acquired the bait that attracted the team to the area in the first place. They
moved into the almost-finished Nassau Coliseum, a
14,800-seat, modern arena. The toilets there were as spa-
cious as the dressing rooms in the Island Garden. In the
new setting, in new uniforms designed by Mrs. Roy Boe,
the Nets acted like a new team. They rallied at the end
of the season to finish with 44 wins and 40 losses and
upset the Colonels, who had won more games in the
regular season than any team in ABA history, in the
first round of the playoffs.

Then they defeated the Squires and their rookie sensation Julius Erving in six games. The experienced Indiana Pacers were too strong for the Nets and defeated
them 4 games to 2 in the championship finals. But the
Nets had moved into a place three times the size of any
home they had ever had and proven that if they could
win, they could sell the place out.

There is nothing better for a growing franchise than
to finish second. Winning a championship often makes
fans complacent; they ignore the regular season and wait
until the playoffs to come out in impressive numbers.

But a team that finishes second encourages their fans, tempts them into believing something even better is coming. And they want to be in on it when it does come. So the Nets had done everything right in 1971–72—acquired Barry, moved into the Coliseum, finished second. The next season held such promise even the most dour rooter couldn't help but enjoy anticipating it.

But during the off-season the net fell out from under them. A California judge ruled that the contract Barry had signed with the Golden State Warriors took precedent over any later agreement he signed with anyone else. It was a bomb as big as the Americans had been in New Jersey.

There was a lot of speculation before the new season that the Nets would be as good without Barry. There was too much talent on the team, the stories said, for a player like Barry to monopolize the action as much as he had. Boe has signed the top college player in the country in the middle of his senior year before anyone else had had a chance to get to him. Jim Chones, a six-foot-ten center from Marquette, was expected to be the new catalyst. He had also acquired George Carter from Carolina, who would pick up the scoring burden at forward. But all the speculation was wrong.

Chones was asked to try to play forward so that Billy Paultz could also be in the lineup at center and both of them were unhappy. Rookie Brian Taylor replaced John Roche as a starter at guard, and Roche was a malcontent. Carter was expected to do everything Barry had done, but he could not, and the contribution he did make was overlooked. The team started losing and feuding, and Carnesecca lost control of the situation. The players started playing for themselves instead of together. And they finished fourth in their division with a record of 30 wins and 54 losses, 27 games behind first-place Kentucky. They were easily defeated in five games of the first round of the playoffs by Carolina.

The worst thing a team can do after finishing second and encouraging their fans is to finish fourth and discourage them. In one lousy season they had undone all the good they had done the year before. So Boe realized that even though his players were off for the summer, he had to keep busy. He had to use the time between May and October to build the kind of interest that usually builds during the season. He had to keep his team in the news . . . and it had to be good news.

8. The Coming of Dr. J.

For the last game of the 1972–73 season the Nets started a team made up of Jim Chones and George Carter at forward, Billy Paultz at center, Billy Melchionni and Bob Lackey at guard. Off the bench for workouts of varying length came George Bruns, John Roche, Brian Taylor, John Baum, and Tom Washington. Seated on the bench were Lou Carnesecca, the coach and general manager of the team, his assistant, John Kress, and Fritz Massman, the team's trainer since their very first game back in the Teaneck Armory.

The opposition that night was the Virginia Squires. Seated on their bench was their coach-for-a-day, Julius Erving. He was filling in for Al Bianchi, who was scouting the Colonels, their opposition in the first round of the playoffs. The Squires won that game, 121–106. "I was just putting in the people who the people sitting behind me were hollering for," said the winning coach after the game.

It was the first game Erving had ever coached in pro basketball. And it was the last game Carnesecca would ever coach there.

Two years earlier Carnesecca and Roy Boe had decided not to sign Erving or ask him to give up a year of college. So the Squires rushed in and signed him instead. And everyone else in the league was also signing any undergraduate they could get their uniforms on. It wasn't long before Carnesecca and Boe realized they had made a mistake. That decision might have been the turning point of Carnesecca's career with the Nets.

By the time Julius put on a Nets uniform for the first time in October of 1973 Carnesecca was gone. So were Chones, Carter, Lackey, Bruns, Baum, and Washington from the last game's lineup. And halfway through the season John Roche would go elsewhere too. Roy Boe was not a man to sit around. He was a man of action. The caper was only the most visible of moves. But Boe bought more new faces than Xavier Cugat.

His first move was the coaching change. His inclination was to bring in someone young and popular to be both coach and general manager. He reportedly offered that combination to Al McGuire, the New York bred coach of Marquette University. McGuire refused to come to the pros for the fifth or sixth time. Then he offered the job to Dave DeBusschere, the thirty-three-year-old forward of the New York Knicks. DeBusschere was a man without the natural talent who had worked until he became the best two-way (offensive and defensive) forward in the league. He was the catalyst that turned a talented Knick team into consistent team and brought them two championships in four years. An he was among the five best-known athletes in all of New York. Boe couldn't have made a more popular choice. But DeBusschere wanted no part of coaching.

At the age of twenty-four he had been made the player-coach of his first pro team, the Detroit Pistons. When he took that job, he decided to give up his off-season job—pitching for the Chicago White Sox. But he did not enjoy the coaching experience enough to return to it. He would accept the general manager's role if Boe would also hire a coach. Boe agreed and gave him a ten-year contract worth $750,000.

Boe then apparently asked DeBusschere to name the best young coach around. Dave named Kevin Loughery, a teammate of his at Detroit and then the coach of the Philadelphia 76ers, the worst team in pro basketball.

From Detroit Loughery had been traded to the Baltimore Bullets in the middle of the 1963–64 season and he established himself as the other guard in the backcourt with Earl Monroe. Loughery was always an ego player. He came down the floor looking to take his own shot first, and then if it were not available, he looked for an open teammate. He managed to average around 20 points a game during his eight years with the Bullets. But the thing he is most remembered for is coming out of the hospital with a brace supporting a collapsed lung and playing against the Knicks in the 1970 playoffs.

Loughery had been traded to Philadelphia along with Fred Carter in the middle of the 1971–72 season for All-Star Archie Clark. Clark was the last of eight All-Stars the 76ers had traded away in the five years since they won three division championships in a row. With the arrival of Loughery and Carter, two competent but unspectacular ballplayers, the team was as exciting as Ed Sullivan.

Roy Rubin had come to coach the 76ers from a job at Long Island University. Rumor had it that he was the only coach in America who would take the job. Rubin's hobby was investing money in Broadway shows. He had a better shot at success there than he did with the 76ers.

By the time the mid-season All-Star break rolled around Rubin had coached the team to a 4-and-46 record and a 20-game losing streak, the longest in league history.

Loughery had come to the All-Star game in Chicago as the vice-president of the NBA players' association. He thought he was playing the best ball of his career until his season was ended early by a knee injury. But he looked forward to an operation at season's end and then three or four more years as a player. At that game Irv Kosloff, the owner of the 76ers, told Kevin that he was firing Rubin and wanted him to take over as coach. They made a verbal agreement that Kevin would finish out the year and become player-coach for the next two. They would sign and make it official later.

"I had always wanted to go into coaching," Loughery says, "but never expected it to happen quite this fast. When I took the offer, I thought I was in a good position. We had a number of top draft choices. And we had nowhere to go but up. Anything I could produce would be an improvement.

"As bad as things were on that team, there was never any dissension among the players. They were all good guys who would work hard. If they were in the right situation they would win. The draft choices could produce that right situation.

"I was getting a player's salary since I was to be a player-coach. The money was too good for me to stop playing if I didn't have to."

But the agreement remained verbal. Loughery's lawyer, Larry Fleisher, and Kosloff never could come to terms on a contract. Kevin finished out the year with the team leading them to 5 wins in the remaining 32 games.

With the college draft approaching as soon as the play-off finals were over with, Boe had to find himself a coach.

On Friday, May 4, Loughery received a call from Fleischer, who is also DeBusschere's agent, asking if he wanted the Nets job. On Sunday he came to New York and attended the third game of the Knicks-Lakers play-off finals at the Garden. On Monday, May 7, Loughery signed a contract to coach the Nets for the next five years at a reported $40,000 per year.

"I took the job because I had found that playing and coaching at the same time was almost impossible. At Philly I couldn't afford to just coach. With the Nets I was being paid well enough for the one job.

"Also if you get a chance in New York, you just have

to take it. That's how I feel anyway. I grew up in the Bronx and went to college in New York [St. John] and my wife is from here. You always want to come back here.

"And then of course there was the security of the five-year contract. That's a tremendous opportunity for a coach."

The next week the Nets signed rookie Larry Kenon, who had established himself as a pro prospect with an outstanding performance against Bill Walton and UCLA in the NCAA finals. And then in June they made the deal for Erving. In a month Loughery had gone from the least desired coaching position in basketball to the most desired. But having spent his whole career in the NBA, he didn't really know what he was getting into.

"I had played a couple of exhibition games against the ABA teams," he says, "but when you're in a league that's been established, you tend to look down on the new league. I'm sure the NFL was the same way with the AFL.

"I had played in exhibition games against Julius and seen him play on TV. I knew he was good. But I never realized how good."

The coach of a basketball team has to decide on a philosophy that his team will adhere to and build according to that philosophy. Many coaches panic and change the philosophy as soon as their teams lose a few games. Those coaches don't stay around too long.

During the summer Kevin Loughery decided his team would run on offense and press all over the court on defense. It seemed to him that that was the philosophy of the teams that were winning most consistently in both leagues. In Erving, Kenon, and Brian Taylor he appeared to have three players whose own styles fit right into this team concept. In Billy Paultz and Bill Melchionni he had two players whose styles did not. Loughery's philosophy demanded quickness on offense and defense, and that was the one attribute Paultz and Melchionni both lacked.

The Nets opened the regular season by winning 4 of the first 5 games. But they were not winning because they were playing together. They were winning on the basis of individual talents. As he had with less talented teams in college and in Virginia, Julius was carrying too much of the load. "We were all standing around looking for Dr. J.," says Brian Taylor. "We expected him to pick up the burden. We expected him to do it by himself. We had no closeness. No rapport. And Julius was distant from everyone."

There were rumors that Loughery was disappointed with the general caliber of ballplayer he had found in the ABA, and Julius was not excluded from this. "You'd never get away with this in the NBA," he would yell at his players. And they resented it.

The Nets lost a close one in Kentucky, 100–98. Two nights later they lost another close one at home to San Antonio, 88–87. The losing streak went on. Three games. Five games. Pride started to hurt. And soon bodies began to hurt, too. The Doctor would not carry the whole team on his back. He was even having a problem carrying himself on his knees. They ached. For the first time in his career. In a game at Utah he could play only twenty-two minutes and contribute 9 points. And the Nets lost their eighth straight.

Loughery was panicking. He was prepared to break the first rule of coaching and change his philosophy. But it was early in the season, very early. And if there was going to be a change, this was the time to do it.

"My original concept seemed perfectly suited to the Doctor," he said. 'He plays so hard, so fast. But no one could play that way for eighty-four games. By the third week of the season I had run him into the ground. I was in the process of destroying the best player on my team, maybe in the game."

On Saturday, November 10, the Nets traveled to San Diego for the first time all season to face the Conquistadors and the biggest coach in basketball, Wilt Chamberlain. They checked into the Ramada Inn, and then all the players were summoned to Loughery's suite for a meeting. The team usually had a meeting on days when they came into town for a one-night stand and had no time for practice. They would go over what they would do in that night's game. But that afternoon the discussion was more general.

"That meeting was the chance for our players and coaches to open up the doors to communication," Julius later said. "The coaches challenged the players and then turned around and pointed a finger at themselves. I was amazed that as young as we were, we had the sense to have that meeting."

"It was a cold, hard meeting," Taylor says. "I remember leaving that room wondering if I was really capable of playing pro basketball. I really was forced into stopping and taking a look at myself. All along I was upset that everyone was so cold. But that meeting was so painful that I left feeling that maybe the coldness was better."

"I told my team that I had let them down," Loughery says, "that I had lost ball games for them. You have to be real with people in this game. The players are hep. You can't con them. I was conned a lot in my career and I didn't like it. I let them know where they all stood. That's the only way."

"It took a lot of guts for Kevin to admit his mistakes to us," Brian said. "But it made us all more honest with ourselves. I think the Doctor was really affected by that meeting. He began to realize his role. Billy Melchionni was the captain, but Doc was going to have to be the leader. On the court and off it."

The closed-door team meeting is a common occurrence in sports. It is no different from any boss-employee or foreman-shop meeting in any business, except for the fact that when the door opens, there are reporters standing there trying to find out what went on. Such a meeting can be run in two ways: The condescending boss speaks down to his employees, chastising them for their wrong-doings, or the sympathetic boss opens himself up and forces his employees to do the same. From the comments that came out of this one, it seems that Loughery took the latter course.

Loughery also made visible changes, symbolic moves that showed his players he was trying to reverse their streak. The night of the meeting he installed John Williamson, a rookie guard from New Mexico State, in the starting lineup. He replaced the injured Bill Melchionni, who had been an All-Star for the past three seasons. Williamson was bulkier and cockier than Mel. That night the Nets lost again to the Q's, 107–105. Nine in a row.

The next day the team was in San Antonio to face the Spurs. But they left the all-court pressing defense in San Diego. Instead they went to a sagging man-to-man, clogging up the middle under the basket forcing teams to shoot up over them from the outside. They beat the Spurs that night, 106–94.

Two nights later they won in Memphis. They won 19 of their next 22 games, including 9 in a row at one point, as many games as Loughery's team had won the entire year before.

"In the beginning of the year I really didn't know how to work the players together," Loughery said. "We had so many new guys that it didn't help for me to study their past on film.

"As we went along, I learned how to use the Doctor. And we began to put things in to utilize his talents."

Up to that point in his career no coach had learned to use Julius' talents properly. At Virginia he would clear a defensive rebound, dribble the length of the court and work for his own shots. It was spectacular basketball. But pro teams don't win with one man doing everything. As Loughery once said, "You still get only two points for being spectacular."

Loughery's original plans to run and press were an intelligent attempt to utilize Julius' abilities. The game would depend on stamina, and in the past it had appeared that Julius could run all night. But he would not be able to keep up the pace over a full season. Loughery was thinking along the right lines by trying to maximize quickness. But his method of implementing his theories was slightly off. The new defense emphasized the same theories without demanding so much of the players. In the sagging, man-to-man defense, a thinly disguised zone, Julius could use his quickness to upset the rhythm of a team that was working the ball around for a shot. He could then slip off a man under the basket to use his rebounding talents.

"On offense we set up plays to have Doc get the ball on the move," Loughery said. "Early in the year we would pass it to him while he was standing still and teams would be able to drop off an extra defensive player on him. But we put more movement into our plays so that he ended up as the last man on the end of a play."

Julius seemed more relaxed in the new system. His body was not taking the physical punishment that had limited him earlier in the year.

By the time the mid-season All-Star break rolled around, the Nets had climbed into contention for first place.

On Sunday, January 20, they hosted the Kentucky Colonels in a game that would determine first place for the moment. The coach of the winning team that day would also be the coach of the East squad in the All-Star game.

With just over two minutes to go in that game the teams were tied at 99. The Nets had the ball on offense and passed it around, looking to get it to Julius standing along the right baseline. When they did get him the ball, most of the players crowded in underneath the basket, expecting Julius to take the long shot, hoping for the rebound if he missed. But Julius did not take that shot. Instead he put the ball to the floor, drove along the baseline into the crowd, went up in the air and wiggled his body in between everyone until he was close enough to dunk it through the basket. The Nets led 101–99.

After a few exchanges the Nets were ahead 103–102. They took possession of the ball and handed it to Julius just beyond the Colonels' foul circle. He dribbled in place to run the thirty-second clock halfway down and then began to move toward the basket. He faked to the outside, then came right down the middle at seven-foot-two Artis Gilmore. He went high up into the air and released the ball for a certain two points. The two that would assure a win. But Gilmore jumped high above the rim and swatted the ball away. "Goaltending," Loughery yelled.

"Goaltending," the crowd yelled.

But the referees ruled the ball in play.

Julius eventually picked up 2 more points on foul shots, but the Colonels picked up 4 and won the game 106–105.

After the game all the Nets stood around the locker room in their sweat-soaked uniforms looking at the videotape of that controversial blocked shot over and over again. No one said a word. They felt they had been robbed of a big win, a win that could have earned their coach an honor. But there was nothing they could do right then. They filed it away in their minds, dressed, and went home.

A game against the Colonels did demonstrate the

Nets' main weakness. They did not have a forward with the muscle to defend a strong opposing forward whose game was using his size to get shots in close to the basket. On that night they were hurt by Dan Issel, a muscular, six-foot-nine player. He pushed his way at will into the position he wanted under the basket. George McGinnis, the burly forward of the Indiana Pacers, would do the same damage to the Nets. Just as when he was in high school Julius' weakness was trying to stop this type of player.

John Y. Brown, the owner of the Colonels, meanwhile felt that his own team needed offensive help at guard. And he had his eye on John Roche of the Nets. Roche was a fine shooter, but was deficient on defense. He was not getting much playing time in Loughery's defense-oriented system. Just before the All-Star break the Nets gave Roche to the Colonels in exchange for Wendell Ladner and Mike Gale. Ladner is a strong, adventurous forward with the strength to fill just the role the Nets needed filled. Gale is an unspectacular but consistent guard who can do everything fairly well and is excellent on defense. Most of the people around the league were shocked by the deal—including Babe McCarthy, the Colonels' coach. He had not been consulted. And his boss had given away the strength of defense to their divisional rival. "Running a basketball team ain't like selling chicken," said one of the Nets.

By the time the All-Star game did arrive, the Nets had moved past the Colonels and into first place with a record of 34 wins and 20 losses. Julius had been voted to the East's starting team. Center Billy Paultz and rookie forward Larry Kenon had been chosen by Babe McCarthy as reserves.

The game was to be played in Norfolk, Virginia, on the court that had been Julius' home the past two seasons. And from the moment he arrived in town he was the center of conversation. The best players from every team were there, but all the talk around the hotel and in the local papers was of how Julius would affect the outcome of the game. McCarthy had three of his own players in his starting lineup, Issel, Gilmore, and Louis Dampier. And yet when he was asked how he approached the game, he said, "My team will run. When you have Julius Erving on your team, you play to emphasize his talents."

While all this talk went on, Larry Kenon sat alone in his hotel room relaxing. He had been overshadowed by the Doctor all year.

Sitting up in the cheaper seats at any arena, looking down on the Nets shooting around before the game, it is easy to confuse the two forwards. They are both black. They are both thin. Although Kenon is listed as three inches taller, with their long Afros they look about the same height. Julius wears number 32. Kenon wears 35.

"I was first linked to Julius Erving when I was still in College [Memphis State]," Larry says. "The public-relations man there, Scoop Grogan, wanted a nickname for me and named me Dr. K. I resented it right away. I wanted my own identity.

"But when the Squires came in to play the Tams, I had to go see this guy I was named after. The night I saw him he looked like he was just coasting. And he still scored 27 points. Now that I'm in pro ball, I know that there are some nights when you just coast.

"After a lot of confusion with him and with me I ended up on the same team with Julius. They didn't want Dr. J. and Dr. K., so someone decided I was Mr. K.

"Actually I was lucky to have him on my team. If he wasn't with these Nets, it would put a lot more pressure on me. I would be expected to do more things. Now he gets the attention, and I can learn to play in the pros.

"There are no set plays for me in the Nets offense, but I don't mind. I still get my 16 or 17 shots a game just by being where the ball is.

"I can't resent his presence. He's good people. Just good people. He's not plastic or false. He's just a natural guy. You got to like a guy like that.

"There's no more comparisons. Not by the players. Not by the fans. I do my thing and he does his, and we're both on the All-Star team. People see what we both do."

That night when the All-Star teams were introduced at Scope, Juius was given the loudest ovation. Kenon was greeted courteously as were the rest of the players. In that game Larry Kenon scored 20 points. Julius just coasted.

Shortly before the All-Star break, Julius announced that he planned to marry Turquoise Brown from Winston-Salem, North Carolina, on Saturday, February 9.

On the Wednesday preceeding the scheduled wedding the Nets played the Pacers in Indiana. Julius enjoyed a superb evening scoring 40 points, and the Nets won easily, 121–100.

A number of the Nets' away games are televised back to New York on a small local television station. The same station that televises a number of the Knicks away games. The day after any Knicks broadcast there seems to be a lot of chatter about the game around town. Despite the presence of seven other teams in the four major spectator sports, the Knicks own New York. And their players are the most heralded sports celebrities in town.

It is difficult to find anyone to discuss a Nets game with the morning after. But on the night of that Indiana game, for no logical reason, everyone you talked to seemed to have watched the Nets. Everyone had seen Julius' great show. And Manhattan was buzzing with talk about the Nets. Talk about what Julius had done on the court. And consequently, talk about his upcoming wedding.

Julius had tried desperately to keep the location of the ceremony a secret. For just the one day, he wanted to free his fiancée and friends of the pain and commotion of an audience.

The night before the wedding the Nets' players threw Julius a bachelor party. And somewhere, sometime, amid the booze and the music, he made the mistake of mentioning that the wedding was going to take place at the Americana Hotel in Manhattan.

Just before noon on Saturday, the first invited guests arrived at the hotel and were greeted by a barrage of newspaper and television cameramen. They were all set up awaiting Julius' arrival. They waited all day. The star never showed.

On the six o'clock news program that evening the local sports commentators reported that those oversized feet of Julius' had gotten cold. He had canceled his wedding.

This was not at all in character for Julius Erving. Anyone who had ever been close to him said that he carefully considered every decision he made. Contrary to his style on the basketball court, nothing he did off the court was spontaneous. If he had indeed decided to get married, he was not going to pull a switch at the last possible moment.

On the eleven o'clock new the same reports were given. No wedding.

The next afternoon, the Nets had a home game scheduled against the Memphis Tams. As the teams ran out on the court for their warm-ups, Turquoise took her usual seat in the first row under the north basket. She wore a wedding band on her left hand.

Upset by the reports of the crowd awaiting him at the Americana, Julius had put on a move. He got together Turquoise and their two closest friends, Dave

Brownbill and his girlfriend Frannie Ryan, and the four of them escaped to a small suite in the Waldorf Astoria. There they waited until Judge Maresta finished another engagement. And around midnight he performed the ceremony with just the five of them in the room. They drank champagne and dined on pretzels and potato chips. It was a far cry from the affair they had originally panned. But they had preserved the most important element—privacy.

Julius scored only 18 points on Sunday, but the Nets easily defeated the Tams, 121–91.

The team was starting to come together now. Ladner and Gale were providing the rugged, physical defense they had been missing early in the season. Everyone seemed to understand his own role in the team concept.

"Julius became less spectacular," Brian Taylor says. "He started looking to us more. He helped us look better and by doing that made himself look better.

"Growing up with a brother like Bruce (who plays football for the San Francisco 49ers), who was older than me and always a star, I was always in a position to envy someone. But Bruce made me confident that I could go as far as I wanted to. What he did for me helped me to get along with other ballplayers. I never resent the presence of a Dr. J. I just try to take advantage of the things he can do for me and for all of us."

"Julius can get 40 points any night he wants to," says Loughery. "But the team wouldn't win as much. He realizes that."

With Kentucky winning almost every night the Nets had no time to relax as the long season neared an end. They won 9 of their last 10 games. They won the Eastern Division title, the team's and Julius' first title of any kind. And they doused themselves and anyone who dared to come near them with champagne after the last game against Denver.

"It's no secret that players like each other when

they're winning and fight when they're losing," Taylor said. "Looking around at the guys in this locker room is very satisfying now. Looking at them and thinking about how they were when the year started. Williamson wasn't playing. Kenon was having trouble adjusting to the big city. Julius had more press around him than ever before. It was a problem, and it mushroomed into bigger problems. But we matured together and learned to handle it. It's nice. It's real nice."

"W.C. Fields was right," Loughery said. "I'd rather be here than Philadelphia."

In professional basketball you play 84 games just to determine who and where you play in the year-end elimination tournament called the playoffs. Which is like suffering through twenty-five years of a first marriage, then getting divoced and remarried to the girl you really loved, because the girl you really loved wanted a man with experience. If you live through the first one, the second one should be a breeze. But this is not the case.

Nothing that happened in the first marriage has anything to do with what happens in the second. And nothing that happened in the regular season has anything to do with what happens in the playoffs.

In 1972 the Colonels had an easy season, walking all over the other teams in the league and losing only 16 games. But they were eliminated in 5 games in the first round of the playoffs by the Nets, who had lost 40.

In 1973 the Carolina Cougars and the Utah Stars were the dominant teams in the league and had the best records in the regular season. But the Kentucky Colonels and the Indiana Pacers were the two teams that made it to the finals of the playoffs.

In 1974 the Nets had the best regular-season record in the ABA, with 55 wins and 29 losses. This guaranteed them an extra home game in each seven-game playoff series. It also allowed them to meet the weakest of the eight teams that qualified for the playoffs, the Virginia Squires, in the first round.

Still, very few people really believed they would survive the three rounds and become the league champions. Experience is supposed to be the key factor in the playoffs. The mature teams supposedly know how to handle the pressure. But actually that pressure exists only when a team has three losses and can be eliminated if they lose one more game or if the teams are tied at three games each, and one game determines who goes home. True, if the young Nets found themselves in a seventh game, they might not have been able to handle the pressure. But no one will ever know. They never hung around for a seventh game. They didn't even hang around for a sixth.

In the first round they easily defeated the Squires in the first two games on their home court. Then they traveled to Hampton, Virginia, and found themselves playing the Squires low-caliber ball. Still they had the ball with only a few seconds left on the clock, trailing by 1 point and needing a basket to win. Julius took the ball, drove down the left side of the court, went up for a lay-up and missed. The Nets lost 116–115. The hometown Virginia fans probably were disappointed at the outcome. They would have preferred to see their favorite player score the winning basket even if he was on the other team.

But the game was a fluke. The Nets knew it and the Squires knew it. And the Nets defeated the Squires handily in the next 2 games to win the series 4 games to 1.

Meanwhile the Colonels were eliminating a strong Carolina team in 4 straight games. The Colonels were the betting favorite in these playoffs. They had been the betting favorite the two previous seasons too, and were yet to win a championship.

But that series against the Cougars only helped con-

vince everyone that they were the dominant team in
the league. Everyone except the young Nets. The major
factor in the Colonels' success is supposed to be the
presence of Artis Gilmore, the best center in the league,
clogging up the middle on defense. You are not supposed to be able to go up the middle against the Colonels. Julius had discovered this in that mid-season game
that determined the All-Star coach. But he still wasn't
prepared to accept the theory. In the first game, he
went up the middle time and again as if there was no
one there, scored 35 points, and the Nets won, 119–106.
A few nights later they won the second game as easily
and went to Kentucky with a 2–0 lead.

A tornado had damaged Freedom Hall in Louisville,
the Colonels' home court and there was some doubt
about when the third game would be played. The arena
was ready by the scheduled day. The team wasn't.

The score was tied at 87 with just seventeen seconds
showing on the clock, and the Nets had the ball. They
gave it to Julius. He dribbled around, but instead of
going to the basket as he had last time, he pulled up
short and hit a jump shot from the corner as time ran
out. The Nets won 89–87. Three nights later they won
again 103–90. They had defeated the highest-rated team
in the league in 4 straight games.

The Utah Stars had also won the first 3 games of
their playoff series with the Indiana Pacers. But they
couldn't wrap it up in the fourth game. Or the fifth
game. Or the sixth game. They did however, manage
to pull together and overwhelm the Pacers in the seventh,
109–87. For this they won the right to come to New
York and play the Nets twice. The Pacers must have
been glad to pass up the trip.

In the first game of the finals nine of the ten players
who took the floor were flat. The tenth, Julius Erving,
took the opportunity to put on a one-man show as exciting as the one Sinatra had put on in the same build-

ing a few nights earlier. Julius scored 47. The Nets scored 89. The Stars scored 85.

When the teams met again five nights later, Julius was not as hot, but everyone else on his team was and the Nets won 118–94. It was their seventh straight play-off win and it seemed as if there was no way they could lose now.

The Stars had them down by 3 points with ten seconds left in the third game. When Wendell Ladner took the rebound of his own desperation shot and passed it to Brian Taylor, who was standing outside the three-point line. Taylor made the shot. The game went into over-time. And the Nets won another one, 103–100.

They lost the fourth game and blew the streak. But the fans in New York didn't mind—15,934 of them showed up for the fifth game at the Coliseum. You could feel in the air from the outset that this was it. Each of the Nets five starters scored more than 15 points. The team scored 111. The Stars scored 100.

A half-inch of water covered the linoleum tiles that lined the corridor under the east stands of the Nassau Coliseum. People walking toward the celebration had to brace themselves against the walls so as not to feel their feet fly out from under them.

The blue door with the Nets logo on it flew open and a splash of champagne in the face greeted those who walked through it. The tall men in the white shorts with red and blue trim (basketball shorts, not jockey shorts) grabbed each new visitor to their dressing room and deposited them, clothes and all, under the open nozzles. Some had come prepared and had changed into shorts and t-shirts. Others, including the commis-sioner of the league, Mike Storen, the owner of the team, Roy Boe, and his PR man, Barney Kremenko, just let the cold water run down their ties and sport jackets. Plastic corks popped out of green bottles that read

Andre's of California, and more of the champagne
landed on heads than in mouths.

"To some people this may seem sophomoric," said
Kevin Loughery, the coach of the team, as he twisted
his white turtleneck sweater and watched the water
fall to the floor. "But I wouldn't want it any other way.
You don't get the chance to act like this too many times
in your life."

The water from his shirt splashed to the floor and
pushed some more of the water covering the tiles out
of the door at the end of the corridor. Out there the
majority of the capacity crowd of 15,934 local fans
mimicked the frenzy in the locker room. It had been
half an hour since their team had disappeared. But they
were in no hurry to let this night end. They hung from
the rim attached to one of the glass backboards until
the backboard shattered all over them. They bounced
the wooden police barricades up and down until they
were each in three pieces. They drank whatever beer
was still available and hugged anyone who would let
them. They had paid to see a basketball game and found
themselves at a party. A careless, drunken party.

There is no real finality in sports. Teams play game
after game, year after year and the same fans root no
matter who the participants may be. But there has to
be some prize awarded at some point to make it all
worthwhile. The league championship is that prize. The
Nets had achieved the ultimate within the boundaries
of their profession.

Roy Boe had bought himself a championship. And
Julius Erving won himself a car as the most valuable
player in the championship series.

Roosevelt, Amherst, and Virginia were behind Julius
now. He was in New York. Frustration and disappoint-
ment on the basketball court were behind him, too. He
was a champion. He had achieved everything he could
possibly achieve within the bounds of his league. He

had accomplished what Seaver and Namath had and, in this area, justified his boss' investment. But only one of the five championship games was on a limited national television hookup. And that game was played in —and therefore blacked out in—New York. Even with a championship in hand, the $4,000,000 deal was still the most widely reported occurrence of Julius' career. The Nets' championship would have little effect on attracting a following for the league. The league was still in trouble.

9. Can Dr. J. Save the ABA

I sat inside the Broadway Theatre in New York enchanted by Harold Prince's 1974 version of the musical *Candide*. The colorfully costumed performers danced all around me to the intricate Leonard Bernstein melodies and transported me into that best of all possible worlds they sang about. For the show's duration I was removed from anything that might be going on outside the darkened theatre.

Then the music stopped. The performers disappeared. And I walked out onto Broadway. I looked up the side streets at the other theatres whose marquees were darkened. Some were covered with leftover logos from shows long closed. I realized that the excitement inside the Broadway Theatre was rare. Too rare. For two hours I had teased myself and forgotten that outside Broadway was lingering.

It would probably never vanish. A New York disc jockey had once told me that there would always be theatre because there would always be some rich people who wanted to put on plays no matter what the risks were. But not enough of them.

Diagonally across the street from the Broadway Theatre sits a dark glass forty-two-story tower. On the very top floor are the offices of the commissioner of the American Basketball Association. In the season in which *Candide* arrived that league had their own hit in New

York—the Nets. But they, too, were only teasing the audience.

While the Nets thrived, the Squires in Virginia were close to bankruptcy; the owners of the Carolina Cougars and the Utah Stars, both former presidents of the league, had lost interest and sought a way out; the owner of the Memphis Tams had just sold his hockey team and was now set upon ridding himself of his basketball team, too; and the owner of the San Diego Conquistadors admitted that he could no longer operate his franchise from a 3,200-seat high school gym and unless he found a facility, he, too, was ready to call it quits. Like the theatre, the league was struggling for survival.

The struggle had gone on for six years. In that time all the founders and original owners had gone on to new things. In fact, Davidson and his cohorts had already started another hockey league and, in 1973, were planning to start a new football league and a tennis league. The men who were the owners as the seventh season approached found themselves in much the same position as the original owners the first year. Dolph's unsatisfactory television contract had now faded away to nothing. Carlson's merger proposal was entangled in the courts and in Congress, and a solution looked far away.

The owners were left with two choices. They could fold, take a beating and avoid wasting any more money. Or they could go it alone and try to strengthen themselves to the point where television and the NBA were begging to join them.

The coming of Julius Erving to New York was certainly a factor in encouraging them to take the latter course. Nothing that had ever happened in their various arenas had ever been nearly as important as signing Julius in that law office. Now, determined to make a go of it, the owners turned for leadership to the man who had built their two most successful franchises and the only executive to remain with the league since its inception, Mike Storen.

"The two best things that ever happened to this league," said George McGinniss, the league's second-best player, "were Julius Erving's coming to New York and Mike Storen's becoming commissioner."

In 1966 Storen had joined the Indiana Pacers as vice-president and general manager after working in promotions for the Baltimore Bullets and Cincinnati Royals of the NBA. He ruled his team like the former Marine captain he was. He did not allow any of the team's owners in the dressing room or near the press table. He prohibited them from talking with the coach about personnel or fraternizing with the players except at parties arranged for that purpose. With the owners in the background, and Storen in the foreground, the Pacers won the Eastern division championship in their second year and the first of three league titles in their third.

In 1970 Storen moved on to Kentucky as president and general manager. While there, he outdid the NBA for Dan Issel in his first year and for Artis Gilmore in his second. In 1972 his team set a league record with 68 wins and only 16 losses.

By 1973 it was apparent that Storen had built the two strongest franchises in the league. Indiana and Kentucky faced each other in the playoff finals that year. And during each of the league's first six years, one of those two teams led the league in attendance.

But during the off-season John Y. Brown, the man who had created Colonel Sanders and told the world to take his chicken home and eat it, bought the Kentucky team. Just as he had made the Colonel the star in chicken, he made his wife, Ellie, the star in basketball. Storen soon sensed he was losing the kind of freedom he needed to run the team and he resigned in August. Within a month he was the league's commissioner.

The Doctor does his high-wire act.   RICHARD PILLING

Julius led Roosevelt (L.I.) High School to the Nassau County Championships . . . and the University of Massachusetts to the N.I.T., but his teams never won a title until he joined the Nets.

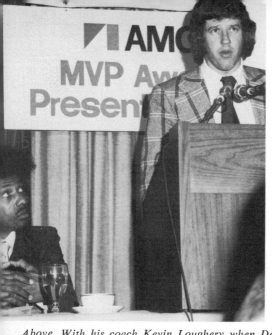

Above, With his coach Kevin Loughery when Doctor J. won the 1974 ABA play-off MVP award . . . below, with his wife, Turquoise.

Assisting teammate Bobby Jones.   RICHARD PILLING

KEVIN FITZGERALD

Now he would try to use the same force that had worked with one owner at a time on all the owners together. He represented new independence for the league. He had not been hired for a specific single-minded purpose as Dolph or Carlson had been. Under him the league would make it on its own. He would not go begging for help anymore than Nelson Rockefeller would go begging for change.

Storen didn't expect any miracles. Above all else, he is a realist. Joe Mullaney, who coached for Storen at Kentucky and quit when the Browns took over, said that Storen was the only boss he ever knew of who wouldn't lie to himself about his team's ability. He would be the same way about his league's.

But his owners would not. In the middle of the season John Y. Brown announced that he was going to effect a merger. Being the man who actually set up such an agreement would be a tremendous compliment to any man's ego. And during the league's first six years more egotists had tried to do it than girls tried to fit their foot into Cinderella's glass slipper. But John Y.'s attempt was in conflict with the image of self-sufficiency that Storen was trying to create for the league.

In the middle of a week in the middle of the season I went to visit Mike Storen in his office, which looks out over all of Manhattan. In his few short months on the job he had already earned a reputation as the most effective sports commissioner since Pete Rozelle of the National Football League.

The job is most delicate in that you are the boss and servant of the same group of men—the owners. They hire you to organize them, and they fire you if you do not run them properly. Most men who assume the role find themselves the owners' tool. But from the outset Storen ran the league just as he had run his own teams. He had a more comprehensive knowledge of the workings of the league than anyone and the gumption to make decisions most men shy away from.

On this sunny day he sat bent over his desk munching at his daily corned beef sandwich, small pieces of which fell onto his stomach, which folded over the blotter. With his small eyes peering from his round, balding head he is both rough and kind at the same time. I knew that he knew that the ability of the league to survive its problems lay squarely on his shoulders. And he would not lie to himself or anybody else about how serious those problems were.

I asked Storen what one player could mean to a whole league. Even one as good as Julius Erving.

He put the remaining piece of his sandwich down on the paper it came wrapped in and picked up a copy of *Sports Illustrated* in his right hand and *The Sporting News* in his left. Julius' picture was on the cover of each. "This is what it means," he said as if he had rehearsed it.

"When we first started this league," he went on, "no one believed we had great players in it. Connie Hawkins started with us, jumped to the NBA and became an All-Star there. With us Spencer Haywood was considered just a kid who wasn't any good. When he went over there, all of a sudden he was a great player.

"We've been saying that Erving is great all along, but no one believed us when he was hidden in Virginia. Then he gets traded to the Nets and they play the Knicks in an exhibition game in Madison Square Garden. The press sees him score at will against Dave De-Busschere and writes that he is the greatest offensive forward in basketball. Now we get the New York press —who I call the national press—on our side. Now Julius is accepted.

"Julius then becomes the standard of measurement. If Dan Issel is battling with him for the scoring lead, he must be a helluva forward, too. If Willie Wise can stop Julius, then he must be a helluva defensive player. If Erving is the best player in basketball—and soon he may be—then everyone else around him looks better, too. You might argue with me, but I think this one player makes for the general acceptance of our whole league. I'm just kind of resentful that it has taken until now for people to recognize him."

A few years ago, when Storen was handling the selection of players for Kentucky, he, too, had paid little attention to Julius Erving. He did not want to hear about a kid from Massachusetts. Then Foreman signed him and Storen got his first look at the kid.

"The Colonels were playing an exhibition game against the Squires in Roanoake. I was the guest on the radio at halftime and I remember saying, after seeing Julius play for just one half, that this kid alone was worth the price of admission. I said that basketball is entertainment, and this kid is the most entertaining basketball player I have ever seen."

But Julius did not have the kind of initial impact around the league that a player of his ability should have had. Having been hidden away before turning pro, he did not have the advance notices of the average pro rookie sensation. "As a drawing card I would say he is the exact opposite of a Bill Bradley," Storen says. "When Bradley went through the league the first time, there was immediate jump in attendance. People all over the country had heard of him and wanted to see him. But he was having his troubles then, probably the worst time he has ever had on the basketball floor. So people did not come out to see him again.

"It was just the opposite with Julius. When he first came into a town, hardly anybody saw him. But those who did spread the word. He put on a super show in Denver his first time there, and the next time he came through, the Rockets sold out."

Julius is obviously the most valuable homegrown

property in a league that has already lost Rick Barry and Spencer Haywood. The attempt by the NBA to lure him away was as big a scandal as MGM's attempt to pull Shirley Temple from Warner Brothers. Like MGM, the NBA was unsuccessful. There has been talk that the owners got together to assemble the package that Roy Boe finally used to lure Julius to New York. If Storen's theory of legitimization is correct, then it was a smart move. But he denies it ever happened that way.

"Boe has always spent money to try to make his business a success," he says. "He brought in Lou Carnesecca, acquired Rick Barry, paid too much money to get him Chones, and now has Julius.

"The whole fight must have cost Earl Foreman $200,000 in legal fees. He is an individual owner. He has no partners. And his team lost $700,000 last year. He had a tremendous financial commitment that he could not meet. He could either keep up the fight for Julius and keep spending or clear himself of his obligations, get Atlanta off his back, and keep Julius in the league. So he traded his star away. I don't think it was a suspect move. But I'm glad it happened. I'm glad Boe could afford the whole thing.

"Now we have Julius on the East Coast and Wilt Chamberlain on the West Coast [with the San Diego Conquistadors]. That could help turn the media around for us. You don't just get Julius and Wilt and have CBS come in and say, 'Now we are ready for you.'

"But now the guys on Madison Avenue will get to know Julius and give him more exposure. And by appearing in commercials and ads he'll get the identity and recognition he deserves."

It seems ironic that the ad agencies could make Julius the national figure that playing basketball had not made him. But often to people in New York the world is no bigger than the island of Manhattan. And it seemed that whatever the people on that island were thinking was the same thing that the rest of the country was thinking. If it were not so, the ad agencies would make it so.

A decade earlier Sonny Werblin, a show-business agent who had once numbered Frank Sinatra among his clients, had taken Joe Namath under his wing and hyped him into a national folk hero. At the time I suspected that although Namath had some obvious charm the buildup was not his doing. There are any number of players Werblin could have drafted for that year and built into what Joe Namath became. Werblin was the master of the Manhattan-hype.

Julius has not yet been taken under the wing of such a master. He has two things against him—he is black and his agent, Irwin Weiner, is also guiding the career of Walt Frazier. There may not be room for two black stars of the magnitude of Frazier, even in New York.

"I'm not saying that one player can make a league by himself," Storen said. "Don't listen to all that garbage you hear about what Namath did. It's good copy, but it's not true. You have to build slowly. Julius is giving us one strong, healthy, well-publicized franchise in the biggest city in the country. Now that's building!"

The phone rang and Storen answered it. It was John Y. Brown, the man who had pushed him out of his job with the Colonels—an ironic move and the best thing that ever happened to Storen and to the league.

John Y., as all his friends call him, had an unhappy player in Rick Mount and didn't seem to be doing anything to make him any happier. Storen strongly suggested that he deal him elsewhere. He gave indications that he could make the deal himself if it were necessary.

The next day Mount was traded to the Utah Stars. Storen was using his muscle on the man who tried to take his muscle away from him.

As the 1974 season ended with the Nets as champions and Julius Erving as the most heralded player the ABA had ever had and Storen as commissioner, the league should have been in its strongest position yet. Instead the 1973—'74 season ended with questions about whether the league would ever begin another season.

Consolidation within the ABA and, ultimately, absorption into the NBA is the only means of permanent survival. In order to hang on until that absorption does come, the ABA regrouped during the off-season. The San Diego franchise signed a lease to move from its 3,200-seat high school gym into the 18,000-seat San Diego Sports Arena. The Virginia franchise was sold by Earl Foreman to a group of wealthy Virginia businessmen, who promised to put some money into the team—something that had not been done since it had arrived in the Tidewater region. The Carolina Cougars were sold to a group of New York businessmen, who promptly announced they were moving it to St. Louis and naming it the Spirits of St. Louis. But the Memphis franchise got the best reprieve of all. They were purchased by a group headed by Mike Storen. Even while serving as commissioner, Storen had reiterated his theory that running a franchise was the most interesting job in sports. So he had his third opportunity to build a franchise into a success.

Tedd Munchak, who had sold his Carolina team, would replace Storen as commissioner for one year and then would assume ownership of a new franchise to play in the new Riverfront Sports Arena in Cincinnati. The league was set for one more year. They hoped they would not have to make their own plans beyond 1975. The NBA would be making the plans for both leagues after that.

10. Doc's Game

Basketball players wear short pants.

They wear no hats or helmets of any kind.

You can see the hair on their legs. And you don't have to wait for a shaving commercial on TV to see their faces.

You can sit closer to the playing area, with no barrier separating you from them, than you can to the performers in any other sport. Sitting there, with your coat off and your legs crossed at the knee, you feel like you know them better than you know any other athletes. They exhibit a personality right there on the court.

That's one of the things I like best about basketball. It's so personal. So friendly.

Just by watching his moods and expressions on the court, you can tell that Jerry West is a nice guy. That Dave Cowens is a tough guy. That Walt Frazier is a cool guy.

Watch Frazier walk. Or watch him lie on the floor for a few minutes anytime he falls. The refs always have to stop the game to wait for him to get up. "They can't start without me," he must say to himself as he sits there.

Julius Erving might be the most expressive of all the pros. He runs up and down the court, his arms and legs moving every which way, but his face never changing. His eyes opened wide. His mouth closed. He is quiet and unemotional. But he has tremendous inner confidence. Beat him to the hoop or push him or hold him. He will never shout you down. He will just quietly go about his business in a very orderly manner. Eventually he will make a move that lets you know what is on his mind. Don't tell them. Show them.

Give him the ball. Clear out his side of the court except for him and the man guarding him. Let him go to work. He expresses himself on the court the same way Marcel Marceau expresses himself on the stage—with his body. That's Doc's game.

Good basketball is a team-oriented game, but at the same time it gives the athlete the greatest opportunity for self-expression of all the team sports. In the school-yard, in high school, sometimes even in college, the game is much more individual. One or two players can so dominate a team that it becomes a one- or two-man game. The smarter pros have realized that you cannot play this way and be successful. In 1973 the Kansas City-Omaha Kings decided to make a superstar of Nate "Tiny" Archibald, a small, talented guard. Archibald would bring the ball up court, run all the plays and take the most shots. He won the league's scoring and assist titles. And his team came in last in their division and close to last in attendance. "They knew they didn't have the talent to compete with the better teams," one NBA coach told me, "so they tried to attract the fans by having a big star. They would have won a lot more games if they spread the emphasis around more."

Despite all the media emphasis on superstars, the best teams are those on which the five players make the most equal contributions. This was the way the world-champion Boston Celtic teams and the New York Knicks, who won world championships in 1970 and 1973, approached the game.

On the simplest level all the players are asked to master the same skills. When the team is on offense, all must shoot and dribble and pass and rebound. And then, without the slightest hesitation, without taking a break to celebrate a score, as they do in every other sport, they must turn around and play defense. They have to battle viciously back and forth, maintaining the same intensity on offense and on defense. They have to keep coming at each other like George and Martha in *Who's Afraid of Virginia Wolf?* To let up for a minute is to break down and let the enemy get the upper hand.

When the five team members get out on the court together, all of them are not equally proficient in all the skills. The role of the coach is to organize the team to emphasize the outstanding abilities of each player.

How the individual players perform within the team framework is called that player's "game." A team's offense is designed to let each of the five players play his "game." A team's defense is designed to prevent the opposing players from playing theirs. You try to "take their game away from them."

In a list of the basic elements that define a player's game, Julius may not seem out of the ordinary. He is only a fair outside shooter, although he has improved each year he has been a pro. He is good but not yet great on defense, although here, too, he is rapidly improving. He dribbles well for a man of his size and he is a smart, accurate passer. Of the basics his outstanding element is his rebounding.

But there are aspects of Erving's game that make him unique. There are things he can do on the basketball court that no one else has ever done. There are reasons why the fans sit at a game, quietly watching him, storing up all their energy, anticipating that moment when he will do something new and original and bring them to their feet yelling. There are reasons why everyone who has seen him comes away telling stories about Dr. J.

Julius is now six-feet-six inches tall, although his Afro

often makes him appear as tall as men listed as six-feet-nine or ten. He is about an inch shorter than the average height for forwards in pro basketball. But when they gave out hands and feet, he must have been in line with the seven footers. He wears a size 13½ glove and the biggest ring size made and a size 15 sneaker. And it's those hands and feet that make him different.

He handles a basketball the way the average person handles a tennis ball. He can raise one arm above other player's two outstretched hands and snatch the ball away as though he's taking a handful of popcorn. Or he can be running at full speed, reach down to the floor, pick up a rolling ball or a bounce pass with one hand and shoot the ball without using the other. Or he can be standing with his defensive man leaning on him, call for a pass from a teammate, reach out one hand and catch the pass like a first baseman catching a throw from third.

He can jump higher than anyone in the game, and he reaches the peak of his jump quickly. He can go up quickly twice in a row, or he can hang in the air while others have already returned to the ground. It often appears that he is not jumping from his knees but just pushing straight up with his ankles.

The hands and the feet naturally make him an outstanding rebounder. The best rebounding forward in basketball. But they also make him a unique offensive player.

"I was only six-feet-three when I graduated from high school," Julius explains. "Yet I always had big hands and could jump, so I learned to be trickier than the bigger guys.

"I like to experiment. I loved to watch guys and what they'd do in an emergency situation. When I practiced, I worked on ways to take advantage of my advantages. I set no dimensions for my game. I decided not to limit myself and I found I could do anything that I had ever seen any guy do—except spin the ball on the end of my finger. I could never do that. But you can't use that in a game anyhow."

When most players leave the ground with the ball, they have already made a decision about what they are going to do. If a defender has gone up with them and their plans are disrupted, they usually throw a wild pass and hope that one of their teammates is standing where the ball is thrown. But Julius' ability to hang in the air for so long lets him make decisions at the height of his jump. He will take off toward the basket, see he has no shot, look around, and drop a pass off to a teammate.

In a game against San Antonio in 1973 the Nets called a time-out with four seconds left in the third quarter. Coach Kevin Loughery instructed John Williamson to take the ball out of bounds and loft it in the air above the rim. Julius was to jump up over the rim and stuff it through (a popular play among teams with an outstanding jumper). Williamson took the ball out, but lofted it beyond the basket. It was heading out of bounds. Julius jumped out of bounds, grabbed the ball with his right hand, while still in the air, looked to his right and then his left before finding Larry Kenon under the basket. He passed it to Kenon, who made an easy lay-up. Most players drive to the basket when they have a clear path or only one man to go around. Julius will drive when all nine other players are congregated under the basket. He has an uncanny ability to wiggle into a crowd and get off a shot over them. He has perfected a shot that Net announcer Al Albert calls a finger roll. This is a shot taken when he has risen above all the other players on the floor and above the rim. Holding the ball underhanded, he flips his wrist and rolls it down into the hoop.

For a man his size he is surprisingly quick. He will stand still while his teammates move the ball around the periphery, lulling his man to sleep, not wasting any movement. Then he will suddenly vanish—slipping behind his man or going up over him. By the time his man has looked, Julius has scored.

And then there is the dunk. People have been dunking the ball for years. Kids do it on playgrounds from the time they reach school age. But Julius has become associated with the dunk as if he had a patent on it. What is unique about the Julius Erving dunk is the approach. He leaves the floor farther from the basket than seems humanly possible. It is as if he is flying to the basket. There is a moment when he is in the air, drifting toward the hoop, when you realize what is coming. You hold your breath. When the ball is slammed down through the metal hoop, either one-handed or with both hands back over his head, you rise to your feet with the rest of the crowd. While the building is filled with noise, the players on the other team must maintain their composure and come down the court to try to score themselves. It's not easy. A dunk by Dr. J. usually disrupts an opposing team's pattern.

"My whole defense against him is to try to stop him from going through his high-wire act," says Al Bianchi. "When he does that, he gets his team excited and your players just want to stop a minute and applaud, too. He doesn't do it to be a showman. He knows it will bring his team alive.

"I'll concede him an outside shot any day. Let him score those all day. But I don't want him to dunk. Once he does that, it's all over."

But Julius loves to dunk. He loves what it does to a game. Early in the 1973 season a photographer from *Sports Illustrated* came out to a Nets game to shoot a cover photo. He approached Julius and asked him if he would dunk one over his head in practice. Julius agreed to do it. But practice went on and he didn't.

As the teams were walking out on the floor for the

opening tap, Julius walked by the photographer and said, "I just couldn't do it. I was too cold, I would have ripped my legs apart. But I'll get you one in the first quarter."

Early in the quarter he stole the ball and dribbled down the floor all alone. He could have laid it in the basket anyway he chose to. He went under the basket and slam-dunked over his head, winked at the photographer, and ran down the floor to play defense.

On defense Julius' game takes advantage of his quickness and jumping ability, too. He usually guards his man loosely, looking to drop off under the basket and be in position for the rebound. "I'm a finesse defensive player," he says. "I steal the ball. Or I block a shot. I don't play head up on a man and lean on him. That's just the kind of coaching I've always had. I learned to play position defense."

He stands around the basket, always looking at the ball rather than his man. He is always gambling. He reaches in and tries to get a hand on any pass. He tries to upset his man's rhythm by making it hard for him to get the pass. Often it leads to a steal. Many times it also leads to an easy shot for the man he is guarding.

In a game against the Kentucky Colonels, Dan Issel got behind everyone on the Nets defense and was running down the court. Lou Dampier lofted a long pass like a quarterback throwing to an end on a fly pattern.

Julius was two steps behind Issel when he caught the ball. They both left the floor at the same time. While in the air, Julius came around in front of Issel and slapped the ball away as the Colonel star tried to shoot.

Julius may be the only player in basketball who is capable of playing all three positions—forward, guard, and center. In pro basketball the guards are usually the quickest players and the best ball handlers. Julius is quick and a good ball handler. The forwards are good

shooters and capable rebounders. Julius is a capable
shooter and an outstanding rebounder. Centers are usually big and burly. They set picks and play with their
backs to the basket. Julius uses his jumping ability to
overcome the height and width of bigger centers and
has played with his back to the basket.

His knowledge of the various positions came early,
as Ray Wilson explained. Since his earliest experiences
in organized basketball, he has had characteristics that
let him fit in at all three places.

Teams use different combinations of players to try
to stop their opponents from running their patterns.
They try to create a mismatch on defense, a taller man
guarding a smaller man, a quicker man guarding a
slower man, to confuse the offensive team. But there is
no player of any size who can force Julius to deviate
from his game.

He can also be called upon by his coach to fulfill
any of the functions that no one else on the floor is ful-
filling. If there are problems in the backcourt, he can
handle the ball. If there are problems in the middle,
he can guard a bigger man.

In one short spurt, in the very last game of the 1973
regular season, Julius demonstrated just how many
things he could do.

The Nets came into that game with a record of 54
wins and 29 losses. The Kentucky Colonels were in
second place with a record of 52 and 30. If the Nets
could win the last game, they would clinch first place
in their division—their first title of any kind—and guarantee themselves the important extra home game in
each seven-game playoff series. If they lost, they might
find themselves in an unnecessary playoff game for the
divisional title on the Colonels' home court.

Their opponents that night, the Denver Rockets,
needed the win just as badly. They had a record of 36
and 46 and where a half game ahead of the last-place

San Diego Conquistadors in the Western Division. A loss would probably have meant losing a playoff berth to a third-year expansion team, an embarrassment to coach Alex Hannum, who had won championships with clubs in both the NBA and the ABA.

Julius had played in all 83 previous regular-season games. This late in the season he should have been able to relax a little and prepare for the playoffs.

Not this night.

At the end of the first half the Nets trailed 51–46. The team was playing good defense, but standing around on offense. Julius scored 23 of his team's 45 points, but almost all of them on shots from the outside, fifteen feet or more. His game is going to the basket and forcing the defense to collapse on him, thus leaving his teammates open for shots.

By the end of the third quarter the Nets were ahead 77–76, and Julius had 31 points, but still mostly from the outside. People who know basketball say his game is inside and he is a bad outside shooter. You never would have believed it that night.

The fourth quarter seesawed back and forth, and Julius didn't score for the first six or seven minutes.

Then he took over. He started going to the basket, making one shot after another. He scored 4 baskets in a row and passed off to teammate Brian Taylor for an easy lay-up for a fifth. But the Nets still led only 98–96 with less than two minutes left. He came down the floor again and hit an off-balance fifteen-foot jump shot for a 100–96 lead.

He took a rebound of a missed Rocket shot and dribbled the ball out through a crowd of hands that reached for it. Instead of continuing unmolested to the hoop, he pulled up short at midcourt and dribbled around for a few seconds to kill time on the clock. With ten seconds left on the thirty-second clock he went to the hoop for an acrobatic lay-up that put the Nets ahead, 102–96.

The Rockets took the ball out of bounds and guard Ralph Simpson dribbled down court. A Net tapped the ball from behind Simpson and it rolled on the floor toward the Rocket basket. Julius and Denver's Al Smith took off in a foot race to the ball, and both dived head-first at it, sliding along the floor, scraping their bodies along the way.

The ref called a jump ball.

The Rockets controlled the tap and worked the ball into six-foot-ten Dave Robisch for a short-range shot. Robisch turned to shoot, and Julius went up and knocked the ball back at Robisch.

The ball bounced on the floor and ten players dove at it.

Julius came out of the pack with the ball and dribbled away the last thirteen seconds of the game.

The Nets won the game 102–96. And a divisional title. Denver went on to lose to San Diego in a playoff for the last playoff spot.

Julius had scored 12 of his team's last 14 points and assisted on the other 2. He finished the night with 43. He had blocked shots, rebounded, and dived to the floor after the ball. Superstars aren't usually known for diving after balls.

Shoot, dribble, pass, rebound, and play defense. He had done them all.

I left Nassau Coliseum that night with new lore for the legend. I couldn't wait to find someone to lay it on. This story was not about a great move that no one had ever seen. This story was about the complete ballplayer playing the complete game under the most important circumstances.

I drove home without the radio on in my car. I just wanted to sit and consider what Julius had accomplished out there on the floor. I had gotten the chills watching him.

I tried to recall other games that season in which I had

felt the same way about his performance. There were a few. One in particular, in which he had single-handedly beaten Kentucky in the last quarter.

But there really weren't as many memories as there were from the Rucker or from Virginia or from the earlier years. I remembered his old coach Al Bianchi telling me earlier in the year that something was wrong with Julius. That he wasn't doing his stuff. The high-wire act.

And yet he was on a team that was more successful that any he had ever played for before. He had won his second consecutive scoring title and had finished among the leaders in every offensive category as well as blocked shots and steals. And he would soon be voted the league's Most Valuable Player for 1974.

All this with less theatrics.

In high school, in college and with Virginia, after Charlie Scott departed, Julius had not played on a five-man team. He was the superstar and too much of the action was built around him. His teams had all been victims of what Dave Brownbill had called court tilt.

But with the Nets it all began to change. Julius learned to fit his game into the team concept. He learned that he could be effective without being as spectacular. He grew as a basketball player.

Some of the reasons were obvious. On the Nets he was playing with more talent than he had ever played with before. It was also the youngest pro team. No one on the starting five had completed four full years of college. At the beginning of the season they averaged 22.4 years of age and 1.5 years of pro experience.

Kevin Loughery had learned to use Julius' talent as no other coach had. Julius was given plenty of room to free-lance but within a disciplined system. And he knew he didn't have to do it all by himself. The closing two minutes against Denver were unusual. In a clutch situation they looked to Julius. Otherwise the burden was shared by all.

A few weeks after that game I went to a press conference at Sardi's. It was called for Julius to announce his affiliation with Spalding Sporting Goods. Julius sat behind a microphone in a green pin-striped suit, moving the basketball from one hand to another as though it were an apple. He tucked a check for $75,000 in his jacket pocket and calmly handled the small press gathering.

As he spoke of his team and his game, he showed a new approach. A new understanding. Loughery sat at the table next to him and probably didn't realize the change in his man.

"I want to learn to play defense differently from now on," he said. "I want to be more physical. To lean on a man. And wear him down.

"Defense is where games are won and lost in the pros. There are a lot of guys on our team who can score 20. If I can play physical defense, I will help the team.

"Of course, I still want the guys to depend on me when we need the big points."

At 23, Julius had made the first decision that turns the flashy college player into the best of the pros, the decision that Dave DeBusschere made early in his career and Kareem Abdul-Jabbar made before 1974.

It was only talk now. And talk is cheapest among sports people. Too often they say what they think sounds good, rather than what they really believe.

But I don't think it's that way with Julius. He doesn't have to say things he thinks are impressive.

Al Bianchi was right. Doc's game wasn't as flashy as it had been in Virginia. But he was winning a whole lot more.

11. The Fans

In 1934 Clark Gable took off his shirt in the motion picture *It Happened One Night* and revealed his bare chest. The man was not wearing an undershirt.

The people in the audience were stunned. Men went home all over America and threw out all their undershirts. Some of them haven't worn one since. Overall sales of undershirts dropped by about fifty percent that year.

In 1972 Wilt Chamberlain came out on the basketball court wearing a sweatband (which in the past had appeared around the wrist) around his head. Suddenly kids on the asphalt courts all over the country were wearing sweatbands around their heads. And teams were attracting fans by having "Sweatband Night."

Sports have replaced Hollywood in America. Athletes have replaced actors as our idols.

In the thirties and early forties three times as many people went to the movies a week as go today. We lived vicariously through the stars. We wanted to look like them and dress like them and act like them.

In the fifties, with television, we brought the movies into our homes. The people who became our idols came into our houses every week.

Then, in the sixties, we got too sophisticated for most of what television gave us on a regular basis. But television picked up on sports. The money that TV pumped into the game made the opportunity for profit more appealing than ever.

Soon we had teams and leagues growing in every decent-sized city in the country and all of them on television. Now we had the best of both worlds. We could sit home and watch our idols on television or go out and see them locally in the flesh.

Sports offered people throughout the country most of the advantages of live theatre, film, and television. It was the quintessential form of entertainment for a country with more money and more leisure time.

Movie audiences continued to drop off. The theater was struggling for its life. And sports were getting more and more attention.

Soon the athletes were transcending the other forms of entertainment. Acting in films and on television. Appearing on other people's talk shows or having their own. Making commercials.

The actors were different from you and me. Too different. And too distant. But the athletes grew up in our towns and performed nearby. The movie stars were the property of Hollywood and sometimes of New York. The athletes were the heroes of every town. Every town had its own celebrities. You could see them in restaurants or in department stores. You could have them at dinners and meetings. There were on television and on your streets at the same time. The perfect heroes for modern America.

Being a fan is a lot more fun now. It is a weekly and sometimes even a daily experience. The long seasons make it this way. The biggest stars could take off their pants now and cause only a minor reaction. Our eyes are on the athletes. They are what all of us wanted to grow up to be.

Julius and Vinnie.
They really have very little in common.

Julius is twelve years old. He attends the sixth grade in a school in Norfolk, Virginia—sometimes.

Vinnie is forty-seven years old. He shows people to their seats in the Nassau Coliseum. Sometimes he shows them to other people's seats.

What they all share in is an admiration for Julius Erving. They're all fans.

I was sitting at the press table at halftime of the ABA All-Star game at Scope. Fans love All-Star games but they are really the worst-played basketball games all year long. They are just an organized, high-priced, schoolyard game. You usually get five shooters on the court on each team. Each one wants to show what he can do and refuses to give the ball to anyone else.

The two teams were on the floor taking their warm-up shots before the start of the second half. And much of the crowd had come up out of their seats and was crowding the perimeter of the court, trying to get a little better look at their favorite stars.

The crowd always does this at a basketball game. The only way to get them back to their seats is to start the second half. The first few minutes of that half are usually played to thousands of backs as the fans scramble to their chairs.

A man in a red usher's jacket walked along the front of the scorer's table dropping a dittoed list of the first-half statistics at each writer's seat. I picked up the sheet and began to look at it. Suddenly I felt a chin digging into my left shoulder.

"How many'd the Doctor get?" a young, tinny voice said into my ear.

I turned my head quickly and saw the small, dark boy jump backwards. He stood there with a big smile on his face, embarrassed. He grabbed a pick out of his pocket and ran it through his hair, just to have something to do.

"Here, you want these stats?" I asked, and he put the pick in his back pocket and took two steps to the table.

"Hey, the Doc ain't havin' a good game," he said. "He's named after me, you know."

"Yeah? Your name's Julius, too?"

"Well, it ain't Doctor," he said, and he turned around and slapped hands with his friend.

"My name's Marty," I said. I reached out my hand and we locked thumbs.

"Hey, Charles. This is my friend, Marty. What you doin' down here at this table?"

"I'm here for *Sport* magazine," I said.

"Yeah? *Sports Illustrated?*"

"No. The other one. *Sport.* Just plain *Sport.*"

"You come here often?" I asked.

"Nah, not anymore. I used to. When Julius was with the Squires. He's named after me."

"I know. You told me. You liked Julius, huh? What do you like about him?"

"The way he jams. Yeah, the way he jams."

The game had started again, and another man in a red coat was pushing the people behind the scorer's table back toward the seats.

"Where are you sitting?" I asked.

He looked around the courtside for some empty seats, but didn't see any. "Up there," he said and he pointed toward the top of the arena.

"Are there any empty seats near you?"

"I don't know."

"Come on. Let's go see."

"Hey, man. You leaving? I'll take your seat," Charles said, and he plopped himself down at the scorer's table. The man in the red coat tapped him on the head and he jumped up and ran up the steps behind us.

As we were climbing, the crowd murmur suddenly became a hush. We turned quickly and saw Julius dribbling by himself, out in front of everyone else, toward the basket. He dribbled underneath the hoop, went up in the air, and dunked the ball back over his head with two hands.

The place exploded.

"God damn," little Julius said, and he ran up the rest of the steps slapping hands with all the people in the end seats along the way.

We got two rows from the top of Scope, and Julius and Charles sat down in their two end seats. There was not an empty one, so I sat on the steps in the aisle. A blond usherette came and asked me to find a seat. Julius and Charles doubled up in one and I sat down next to them.

I began to ask Julius questions. He answered everything. I asked him without for one second taking his eyes off the court below.

"Where do you live?"

"Across the street."

"Across the street?"

"Yeah. In the project."

Between the ultramodern Scope and the thirteen-story Holiday Inn, I had never realized there was a project.

"What does your father do?"

"Delivers mail."

"Does he like basketball, too?"

"Nah. He likes beer."

I couldn't tell if the kid was trying to be cute or if he was telling me the truth.

"Do you play much basketball?"

"Jus' 'bout every day."

"Where do you play? In the schoolyard?"

"He don't go near the school," Charles said. "They might catch him."

"What you saying that for, Charles?" Julius said. "Don't you tell my man Marty those things. He thinks I'm a nice kid. Don't you Marty, huh?"

I laughed.

"Who's your favorite pro?" I asked.

"The Doctor, man. I told you. He's the best. And he's named after me."

"You told me that twice."

"Well, it's true."

"Are you as good as him?"

"What kind of things are you askin' me. I ain't no Doctor. But no one is. Not George Gervin or Artis Gilmore. No one."

"Do you want to be like him?"

"Everyone at the project wants to be like him. We go out there to play, and we call out names of who we gonna be today. The first kid to shout always says, 'I'm the Doctor.' Everyone wants to be the Doctor."

"If someone else is the Doctor, who are you?"

"Oh, Charlie Scott or George Gervin. It don't matter. If you're not the Doctor, you're nobody."

"How do you think he got so good?"

Julius didn't have a quick answer for this one. He sat there with a big smile on his face thinking of some smart-ass thing to say.

"Probably by cutting school and just playing basketball."

Now the boring All-Star game was a blast. I was loving it. Every time Julius Erving got his hands on the ball I turned to watch the two kids. They would jump up to their feet and spread their hands apart, ready to clap at anything he did. The Doctor was not having a particularly good game. But they didn't care.

The game ended and I had to go down to the locker room to talk to some of the players.

"Listen, you two," I said, "go down to the floor and stand behind the barrier there as close to the locker room as you can. I'll try to get the Doctor to say hello to you."

"Shit. You ain't gonna do that."

"Look. I'll try."

We began following the crowd down the steps toward the floor level.

"Hey, Marty. You gonna write about me?" Julius asked.

"Never can tell, Julius."

I went into the East team's locker room and tried to find something intelligent to ask the players. I always hated the locker-room interview. What could a player tell you immediately after running up and down the court for forty-eight minutes? That's why I liked working for a monthly magazine. I could get players in a relaxed atmosphere, away from the stadium, where they could relax and think a little.

I saw Julius was just about dressed in his yellow pants and shirt and so I walked outside to station myself near where the kids were supposed to be. But I couldn't find them.

I found Dave Brownbill and tried to describe the two of them, but he hadn't seen anyone like them.

I don't know why they cut out. I really felt let down. They had given me such a good time during the game I wanted to pay them back. I never got the chance.

I was sitting at the press table on the floor level of the Nassau Coliseum one December night watching the Nets manhandling the Memphis Tams. The night before I had watched the Nets walk all over the same team in their own arena, beat them by 17 points.

The Tams were a team of rookies and other teams' rejects thrown together at the last minute by irascible Charles O. Finley. That's the same Charles O. Finley who owns baseball's Athletics in Oakland, who used to own hockey's Seals in California, and who ran all three teams from his insurance office in Chicago. It seemed that business was getting to be too much for ol' Charlie. He was having health problems and marital problems and just didn't have the time or the strength to devote to operating all his franchises. So Charlie sold his hockey team back to the league and was prepared not to open his basketball franchise for the 1973–'74 season. That's right. Not open the team, just as if it were a restaurant. Well, Commissioner Mike Storen put the clamps on the man, and he decided to get it all going a week before the season was to open. The team had always played poorly. But with so little time to get going it was worse than ever.

When a good team plays a bad team, the caliber of play is closer to that of the bad team. The bad team runs recklessly around the floor on offense and fouls carelessly to make up for poor defense. The good team cannot get its rhythm and run its patterns. And the game becomes a sloppy, boring, run-and-shoot affair. That particular night the Nets opened up a big lead and the Tams acted like they couldn't wait to get back to the hotel to go to sleep. At intermission I decided to take a walk and began wandering up the steps toward the top of the building. Seating at the Coliseum is very steep. The highest seats are not very far from the floor laterally, but are so high up that the players below look like pieces in an electric football game. I walked to the uppermost walkway, behind the very last row of seats, and began walking around the oval-shaped arena.

As I approached the section parallel with the end of the court, a deep, rough voice said to me, "Hey, buddy, can I see your ticket?"

"I don't have a ticket. Just passing through," I said.

"What d'ya mean you don't have a ticket? How'd ya get in if you don't have a ticket?"

I told him I was with *Sport* magazine and that I was so bored with the game I had decided to take a walk.

"You think you're bored now," he said, "you shouldda been here before they got Doctor J. At least he puts on a show. Last year I had to fight myself from falling asleep before the game ended. And with as few people as we had up here, if I fell asleep, I probably wouldda been here all night. My wife wouldda never believed that I spent the night in section 332 at the Nassau Coliseum. Would yours?"

"I know what you mean," I said and asked the usher to sit down with me in the last row. He said he couldn't sit down even though there was no one in his section. So I stood with him and talked.

He told me his name was Vinnie. He was forty-seven years old, married, with two kids ("a fat kid and the prettiest girl anyone has ever seen"). He lived in East Meadow, the next town over from Uniondale, where the Coliseum is located. He said he had been working there since the place opened in 1972 and had seen every game the Nets had played in the place.

"I was never that much of a basketball fan. Football was my game. Up here everyone's friendly. They don't tip as well as down there. But they're all friendly.

"I used to watch this kid Julius come in with the Virginia Squires. They loved him here cause he's from Long Island, I guess. Not many athletes from Long Island, you know. Jimmy Brown and Matt Snell and not too many more.

"So, anyway, they all loved him, but I never watched that closely. I just looked at the clock and waited till it was time to leave. The team wasn't going anywhere. And no one was coming. The better the team does, the better I do. And when the team makes the playoffs, the real crowds show up. That's when I clean up.

"Two years ago we beat Kentucky in the first round. Rick Barry was the star then. He missed a game when the team filled the place up. And they beat Kentucky anyway. That was the best night I ever had here. This year they should get to the playoffs again, and maybe I'll have a bigger night. Maybe not."

"So, anyway, this year the Doctor comes in here. I read about it during the summer, and I didn't think too much of it. But some of the guys who like basketball tell

me this is the best kid who ever played anywhere. And
I was here to see him play every night. I figured I better
get to like the game. People are paying good money to
see this guy.

"So, anyway, I began to watch him from the very
beginning. Now, I don't pretend to know that much
about the game. Ask me football and I can tell you anything. That Namath's a bum, y'know. Won once and
everyone loves him. They oughtta get rid of him.

"So, anyway, I began to watch this kid every night,
and I really enjoyed it. I started talking to the guys
about it and I learned a little about basketball. The kid
jumps so high I think some night he's going to go up
for a rebound and shake my hand up here on the way
down.

"There was a kid up here one time. Last week I think.
Against Kentucky or one of those teams. So, anyway, the
kid tells me he goes down to the park and watches these
guys in the summer, and once Julius ripped the backboard right off the pole. Then he said someone told him
that Julius takes pennies off the top of the backboard."

I told him that was an old story they've been telling
for years about players who jump well. He said it might
be, but he could believe it about Julius.

"But this kid is really the greatest. Look how much
this team has won. I really like coming here now. I even
watch the games on TV. Sometimes I even watch that
other team."

"That other team?" I asked.

"Yeah, the Knicks."

"That's the first time I ever heard anyone ever call
the Knicks the other team," I said.

"Well, you oughtta come out and see Julius some more.
He's the best player around. I haven't seen anyone as
good as he is.

"One of the ushers. Black guy. Over there. He says
Julius is high-flying and mystifying. Sometimes those

black guys really know how to say things. That's Julius, all right. High-flying and mystifying.

"I told my kid that. He went and told all his friends. Now they all come in and say, 'Hey, you're the one who said Julius is high-flying and mystifying.' I say, 'Yeah, that's me.' Actually it was that guy over there. But I told the kids, didn't I?"

I asked Vinnie if he drinks Dr. Pepper.

"You're asking me that 'cause of the commercials the Doctor does, aren't you?" he said. "Told you I watch them on TV. Perfect match there. Doctor J. and Doctor Pepper. I like the commercial."

I asked him if he wears undershirts.

"What kind of question is that?" he said. "What does this have to do with the interview. Of course I wear undershirts. Doesn't everybody?"

"Clark Gable didn't," I said.

I hoped he would ask, "What team did he play for?" What an end to the interview that would have been.

He didn't.

"I never saw much of him," he said. "Never went to the movies much. I didn't know that he didn't wear undershirts."

"That's just an old joke," I said. I thanked Vinnie and went back down to the floor, where the Nets were finishing up a 131–91 win.

I didn't bother to go into the locker room that night to talk to the players. I had spoken to the fans. You don't hear much from them. But they have a lot to say.

12. Me and Julius at the Plaza

On an unseasonably warm May morning, a chauffered blue Cadillac limousine pulled up in front of New York's Plaza Hotel. The door swung open and Julius Erving, impeccably dressed in a three-piece blue pin-striped suit, stepped out. He was greeted by John Havlicek, the popular star of the NBA-champion Boston Celtics. As the two tall men linked hands, a horde of newspaper photographers and television cameramen crowded around them to record the meeting. They were both there to accept American Motors cars presented to them by *Sport* magazine as the Most Valuable Players in their league's championship playoffs.

The two stars posed for pictures together, were interviewed together, and sat at the dais for the day's luncheon together. The New York press treated them as stars of equal magnitude. But New York was the only city in which this would happen. Havlicek was a nationally identifiable hero. Julius was still primarily a New York personality.

Havlicek had won his honor in seven nationally televised contests against the Milwaukee Bucks, a team that featured Kareem Abdul-Jabbar, who at seven feet four was the dominant player in the game. The very bitter, very even series had attracted more attention than any previous pro basketball playoff.

Julius had won his honor in an easy five-game series against a faceless team from Salt Lake City. Only one

142

of those contests was televised, and that one was played in the Coliseum and therefore blacked out in New York. The Nets were the only New York winter sports team to win a championship, but their victory was celebrated as unobtrusively as Arbor Day.

Julius had achieved everything he could possibly achieve in one season. He had won the league's scoring championship, been among the leaders in every offensive and defensive category, had won the regular-season and playoff MVP awards and led his team to the championship. He had asserted himself as one of the nation's major sports talents. But he was not yet one of its major sports heroes.

The legend had come a long way since that day I first saw him at Roosevelt High School and then in the Rucker playground. But it had not spread far enough. Havlicek was a television star. Julius was still just a basketball star.

On that day in the Rucker playground I had been upset when I realized that everyone shared my feelings about Julius. Now, seeing him at the Plaza, I was upset that more people did not share my feelings. And yet, *he* was not upset at all. He had had the opportunities along the way to be in the places that would have made him as prominent as Havlicek. He could have gone to a Big Ten school and he could have played in the NBA. But he had decided otherwise. And he is not the kind of person to look back and regret any of his decisions.

There are only two ways really to get to know someone: marry them or to write a book about them. And over the year that I delved into Julius' life I had grown to feel as close to him as to any member of my family. I wanted more for him just as you always do for your family. He had made me like him even though he was in opposition to this project from the beginning.

I had met Julius quite a few times in between the Rucker tourney game and the time I was enlisted to research him. Most of the time it was as part of a group in a locker room or on an outdoor court in the summer. A writer always thinks he knows an athlete better than the athlete knows him. It is natural. We know everything about them from reading about them. They usually know of us only what we tell them. Usually they're not very interested.

As soon as I agreed to do this book, I wrote a letter to Julius explaining to him just what my plans were. It was not to be an authorized book, and therefore Irwin Weiner advised him to give as little help as possible. But I didn't want to sneak around behind his back and have him find out secondhand about what I was doing. I explained in my letter that I was going to talk to people who were close to him. I hoped that he would be flattered by the whole idea.

A week or so after I had mailed the letter I went out to see the Nets play. Actually I went out there to see Julius in the locker room after the game. I was nervous about the whole thing. Throughout the game, I rehearsed to myself what I would say to him. It was like getting up the nerve to approach a strange girl seated at a bar.

The game ended and I followed the rush of reporters into the locker room. I waited until the crowd around Julius' locker disappeared and I approached him.

"Doc, I wondered if you got my letter?" I asked.

"No, I didn't. What letter?" he said.

Now I really was on the spot. I didn't have to come out here after all. I could have saved it for another night. Now I had to explain the whole project to him verbally.

"Well, I sent it to your mother's house," I said. "Irwin Weiner gave me that address."

"We're just back from a road trip and I haven't been there yet. I guess it's waiting for me. What's it about?"

"Well, you see, Doc, I am going to do this book about you. It's kind of an unusual book. It's about what effects you've had on all the people you've been involved with. I plan to go out and talk to all your old friends and coaches. I'm setting out to research the legend of Dr. J."

"Are you asking me if you can do this or are you telling me you're going to?"

"Well, I have a contract, so I guess I'm telling you."

"Well, then, I guess there's nothing I can do about it," he said and he turned and walked into the shower.

When you do an unauthorized book, you are not supposed to expect the cooperation of the subject. I don't know why I expected it to be different this time. Now I knew it wasn't going to be. So I went out and began to research the book. I tracked down all the people I wanted to interview. My only fear was that Julius would tell people not to speak to me. But that was not the case at all.

When I did have occasion to see Julius, he was cordial but distant. I knew he was uneasy about talking to me, so I didn't press him.

I would see Dave Brownbill out at the Nets games, and he would say that he and Julius were talking about the book. And Julius' fiancée, Turquoise Brown, whom I was never formally introduced to, would greet me whenever she saw me. So I figured he was interested in what I was doing even though he didn't want to cooperate.

The more I spoke to people who were close to Julius the more I liked the guy. I began to worry that the book was going to end up too favorable and make him sound better than any person is. But that's Julius. No one ever says anything bad about him.

I discovered a strange thing about the people who were important to him. At the time the stories and anecdotes they told me had occurred, these people had been filling a need in Julius' life. Ryan, Moseley, and Wilson were acting like the father he lost early. He was fortunate to have three men who were so interested in everything he did and who were always there for him to talk to. Most people are fortunate if they have one such confidant. Brownbill was a devoted friend and would stick by him in any circumstances. Leaman and Bianchi were mentors who had helped him mature in his game. But each spoke in terms of what knowing him had done for them. They had all become fans.

I guess this is a natural occurrence when someone we have known all our lives becomes a celebrity. It may happen that reminiscences are all we are left with. The celebrity turns his back on us. But this was not the case with Julius. He was still close to all these people. As I heard them talk about him, I regretted that I was not closer to him. It's hard not to like Julius.

At one point in my research I decided it was necessary for me to speak to Mrs. Lindsay, Julius' mother, since she was such an important influence on him. But I didn't think it was right for me to approach her without first asking Julius. So I went out to a Nets game for another night of waiting-till-it's-over-to-speak-to-Julius.

That night the Nets lost a close game to the Indiana Pacers. In the last few minutes Julius had made a couple of key mistakes that had cost his team the game. He sat on his chair in front of his locker with his head hanging. But I had come out to ask him a question, and like the fool I sometimes am, I went ahead and asked, "Would you mind if I spoke with your mother?" I said.

"I don't think it's a good idea," he said. He was more depressed than I had ever seen him, and I couldn't pursue the matter. This time I knew I had really blown it.

I drove home from the game upset. But I just made up my mind that there was enough material floating around without having to talk to Mrs. Lindsay.

I guess Julius was being as cordial as he could be considering he objected to what I was doing. His team was winning and he was getting a lot of attention, but he was still cordial to everyone. He was as responsive to the fans who clustered around him as he was in earlier days in the parks. He was struggling to avoid having the notoriety change any of his life.

He was always looking out for his mother. He wanted to buy her a new house, but she refused to leave her friends in Roosevelt. No matter how much money he made, she said, she would always be the same.

He was always looking to help out in the community. He came back to play in the Rucker year after year because he had gotten so much out of it before he was a star, he felt he owed it to the people there to give to it now that he was an attraction.

On the day before the Nets were to begin their final playoff series against the Utah Stars he walked five miles in a walkathon for Cerebral Palsy, played basketball with the inmates at a Nassau County prison, and then attended his team's practice.

While in a position of attractive availability to women all over the country, he fell in love with a girl who had an infant son from a previous marriage and lovingly embraced her situation. A few months later they had the first son of their own, Julius Winfield Erving III. He at no time tried to hide any of his life. He never had any worries about what people would say. He was too secure and too considerate for that.

People didn't say nice things about Julius Erving just because he was a star. People were sincerely flattered to have been acquainted with him.

In early May I traveled with the Nets to their final playoff series in Utah. I thought it would be my final opportunity to confront Julius. By then I had spoken to everybody I was going to speak to about him. He knew this. I hoped he would want to have the opportunity to set the record straight.

On the plane trip to Utah I walked up into the first-class cabin where the players were playing poker. Julius was sitting there with a pile of money in front of him, wearing a cap, listening to music through an earplug attached to his portable tape recorder. He likes to bring along his own music when he travels.

I leaned over and said, "Doc, how about if we have dinner together tonight?"

"I'm gonna sack out as soon as we get to the hotel," he said.

"Well, how about tomorrow night?"

"Dinner may be hard. Why don't you just come by the room?"

"Fine," I said and turned quickly to walk back to my seat.

"Say, Marty," he called after me, "what do you want to talk about?"

Now I knew I was in trouble. "Oh, just some things," I said.

"I hope it's not for your book. I'll talk to you about anything if it's not for your book."

"But, Doc, anything I talk to you about is going to be for the book."

"Well, then, I guess we're not going to talk."

I knew we were going to be cooped up in a hotel together in Salt Lake City for four days, so I didn't argue with him there. I would wait for another chance.

The next night the Nets beat Utah to take a 3–0 lead in the series. They won when Brian Taylor made a three-point basket to send the game into overtime. After the game all the Nets sat around relaxing on their chairs in the locker room. Julius was tucked into a corner, hidden by a rolling backboard. I waited for the reporters surrounding him to leave, and I approached him once again.

"Look, Julius," I said, "I want to discuss this thing with you once and for all. I feel kind of funny about the way we have been acting toward each other, and I think you do, too." I felt as if I were talking to a high school sweetheart again. The words sounded so wrong. But I plodded along.

"I am not doing anything evil to you. I am writing what is turning out to be a very flattering book. I wish you were flattered by the whole thing. I have spoken to so many people close to you that I feel as if I knew you as well as I know any of my friends. And they all say such nice things that I wish I knew you better. I don't want you to hate me for doing this."

"I don't hate you," he said. "I don't hate anybody. I'm just listening to the advice of my business manager. He told me not to cooperate. He said it would hurt me financially, and we would eventually do our own book. So that's it."

He was straightforward. As always. And I felt like a criminal. I felt like I was doing something unethical.

When the luncheon at the Plaza was over, I escorted Julius out of the hotel to the limousine waiting to take him to an award ceremony at the Hempstead Town Supervisor's office. As we walked across the street from the hotel, Pete Axthelm, the sports editor of *Newsweek*, came running out of the revolving door. Axthelm had written a book called *The City Game*, in which he recorded and interpreted the legends of playground basketball.

"Julius, Julius!" he yelled like a young fan. "You know all those crazy moves all the kids talked about in *The City Game*, moves no one really ever did? Well, you did them all. Just fantastic."

Axthelm walked away shaking his head, and Julius swung his long legs into the blue limousine, which matched the color of his three-piece suit. He looked comfortable in that suit in that car with dark glasses on. Like a movie star. A tall movie star.

I stood at the side of the car, holding the door open the way fans always did for the stars. I was thinking of just what to say.

"Look, Doc," I finally said, "soon I'll be finished with this book. Then we can sit down and talk to each other casually like friends."

"Yeah, let's do that," he said. He winked and closed the door, and the limousine drove away.

13. A Short-lived Dynasty

The American Basketball Association annually requires each of its teams to indulge in one month of pre-season competition, seven months of regular season competition, and one month of post-season competition before determining its champion. When this period has expired, there is one lasting result—one team wins, all others lose.

But within these nine months, a series of individual dramas of varying lengths are enacted. As in a novel or a symphony, there are flurries and lulls, emotional highs and emotional lows. For each team there is a surviving past, a new beginning, a motif, a turning point, a climax, and a denouement. When the season has ended the elements of which it is composed are too often forgotten and only the end result is sustentative. And yet, if you take time to dissect and analyze that season, as you would a novel or a symphony, you find that each of the elements contributed to the end result. Things that seemed unimportant when they occurred are vital in retrospect.

The season that followed that in which the Nets won the championship was far less satisfying than the previous year, and yet, much more dramatic. The past was jubilant, the new beginning was optimistic. But the motif that developed was frustration, the turning point was shocking, the climax was disappointing, and the denouement was dreary. There was also an epilogue. It was tragic.

Julius Erving was exhausted when his most fruitful season (1973–'74) ended. He had performed in all 97 of his team's games despite painful knees that were continually aggravated by his high-jumping, aggressive style of play. There was speculation throughout the season that his knees would need surgery once it was over. But too often athletes' knees had been further damaged rather than cured by surgery and Julius wanted to avoid it if at all possible. Willis Reed, the center who led the New York Knicks to two NBA titles, and Gale Sayers, the accomplished running back for the Chicago Bears, were two athletes whose careers ended prematurely after knee surgery. The doctors advised Julius to spend the entire off-season resting his knees. He was to play no summer basketball on asphalt playgrounds. Instead, he was to make weekly visits to the Hospital for Special Surgery in Manhattan. There his knees were treated with an electro galvanic stimulator and cybex isokinetic exercisers.

The Nets' management, which had been so active during recent off-season dealing for players to help them win, was equally dormant following the championship year. They signed one draft choice who might help the team, Al Skinner, from Julius' alma mater, Massachusetts, and acquired a free agent, Ed Manning, who had had experience in the NBA.

But while the Nets basked in the satisfaction of a successful season, the other ABA teams strengthened themselves for the coming year.

—Tedd Munchak sold his Carolina franchise to a group of New York businessmen who located the team in St. Louis, renamed it the Spirits, and spent close to three million dollars to acquire rookies Marvin Barnes from Providence College and Maurice Lucas from Marquette. Munchak then replaced Mike Storen as the league's interim commissioner.

—Larry Brown, the coach of Munchak's team, and Carl Scheer, the general manager, took those same jobs with the Denver Rockets, who became the Denver Nuggets. They brought all-star guard Mack Calvin with them and signed rookie Bobby Jones from North Carolina.

—Storen took over the Memphis franchise, changed the nickname from Tams to Sounds, hired his friend Joe Mullaney as coach, and traded with Indiana for Roger Brown, Mel Daniels, and Freddie Lewis, all who starred for the Pacers when Storen ran that team.

—The Utah Stars lost Zelmo Beaty, who jumped back to the NBA, and Willie Wise, who wanted a new contract, but acquired Moses Malone, the most talented high school basketball player since Lew Alcindor.

—John Y. Brown, the owner of the Kentucky Colonels, fired his coach Babe McCarthy, who committed the crime of finishing second instead of first, and replaced him with Hubie Brown, formerly an assistant coach for the Milwaukee Bucks of the NBA. Brown also acquired guard Bird Averitt from San Antonio and forward Wilbert Jones from Memphis.

With the Indiana franchise moving into a new 18,000 seat arena, San Diego moving from a 2,500 seat high school gym to the 15,000 seat San Diego Sports Arena, and San Antonio having firmly established themselves the year before, the league seemed to have more competitive teams and more potentially solvent franchises than ever before. Only Virginia, a talentless team in a small market, appeared to be a weak sister.

Still the Nets were the league's cornerstone. They were located in the vital market, they were the defending champions and, in Erving, they had the league's biggest attraction.

At the season's outset, the Nets were weakened slight-

ly by injury. John Williamson had had off-season surgery
to remove bone chips in his knee and he was not fully
recovered, and Wendell Ladner had hurt his back and
could not play. Julius was well rested and relieved that
he did not undergo surgery. Early in the season, the
players are fresh and can play for long periods of time.
By mid-season, when the schedule got rugged and the
players were tired, the Nets expected to be back at full
strength.

Three weeks into the season, they went on a four-
game road trip on which they got their first feel for the
new shape of the league. They defeated a muscular but
inexperienced team on their first visit to St. Louis. They
defeated San Diego in their new home. They lost a
physical, quick-paced game to Larry Brown's revamped
Denver team. And they beat Utah and Moses Malone.
Before that game at the Salt Palace in Salt Lake City,
Bill Daniels, the Stars' owner, asked Julius if he would
make a speech at mid-court officially welcoming Malone
to the league. The season was three weeks old and the
Stars had already played three home dates, but Daniels
thought it appropriate to wait for Julius to come to town
to welcome his rookie. Julius was, after all, the symbol
of the league, its best known star, and ambassador of
good crowds.

Two weeks later, the Nets traveled to Kentucky to
play two games in four nights against the Colonels, one
in Louisville and one in Lexington. The Nets-Colonels
rivalry had replaced the old Kentucky-Indiana rivalry as
the most intense in the league. The combined appeal of
Erving and Muhammad Ali, who was honored at half
time, attracted over 16,000 people to Freedom Hall
where the Colonels won 103–97. Three nights later, the
Nets blew a five point lead in the last 30 seconds and
lost in double overtime, 132–129. Julius scored 44 points.

In the first month of the season, the Nets had already
seen enough of the other clubs to know that Kentucky

and Denver were the two teams who might supplant them as champions. They quickly found themselves five games behind the Colonels in the loss column, but they had won two thirds of their games playing listlessly. Lethargy is common to teams coming off a championship year. Loughery expected it to dissolve with time.

There was some discontent on the team, particularly from Billy Melchionni, the captain and oldest player at 30. Melchionni had been an all-star just two years before, and now he found himself relegated to the fifth guard on a team that usually played only three. He asked general manager Dave DeBusschere to trade him to a team on which he could play regularly. The Spirits wanted him, but the Nets were not satisfied with what they had to offer. No deal was made. Instead, St. Louis acquired Freddie Lewis from Memphis.

The Spirits visited the Nassau Coliseum for the first time in mid-November. Some 10,000 fans showed up to see Marvin Barnes, the highest paid, most publicized rookie in the league. But Barnes did not show up to see them. He had signed a $2.1 million contract that included a $100,000 bonus. He reportedly had already blown the bonus. He had bought himself a $15,000 Cadillac and then traded it in and bought a $35,000 Rolls Royce. And that was one of his thriftier moves. Barnes was broke. He found a sympathetic ear in Marshall Boyar, a players' agent, who convinced him that his position was due to a faulty contract. So he jumped the team. He was found a few days later in a pool hall in Dayton. He was convinced to rejoin the team. But the trouble with the league's prize rookie was the metaphor for the unrest and problems that would crop up all over the league in December.

As autumn turned to winter, the pre-season optimism vanished like the leaves on the trees. Indiana Pro Sports, the company that owns the Pacers, had also taken on the responsibility of a WHA franchise and management of the new ten-million-dollar arena in Indianapolis. Now the Pacers, the most successful franchise during the ABA's eight-year existence, were reportedly broke and would fold unless new owners were found.

Also, some of the backers who had promised money to Mike Storen in Memphis had not come through, and he too was searching for a way to stay in business.

"I heard you are struggling a bit," I said to him at midseason.

"I'm not struggling," he said. "I'm dying."

Leonard Bloom, the flamboyant dentist who owned the San Diego Conquistadors, ran out of cash, and the league had to take over the operation of his franchise.

While Barnes returned to St. Louis, Joe Caldwell, a perennial all-star, was suspended by the Spirits, and Willie Wise, another perennial all-star, still refused to join the Stars.

The papers were filled almost daily with reports of new problems, reports which when lumped together gave the impression that the league might not survive the year.

While the rest of the league floundered, the Nets seemed to regain the form they had at the end of the previous year. As at the beginning of the previous season, Loughery had expected that his team would run a fast break offense. But the key to initiating a fast break is rebounding, and the Nets were out-rebounded in 18 of their first 22 games. Julius, though averaging close to 30 points a game, was suffering from swollen knees and was having trouble leading the break. So Loughery decided to switch again to a slower, deliberate, controlled offense. The immediate result was a ten-game winning streak, the longest in the team's history, that included wins over both major rivals, Kentucky and Denver, at the Nassau Coliseum. The streak, however, ended with one of the most inept performances in the history of the franchise. an 83–77 loss in Utah in which the Nets scored fewer points than any Net team ever had in a game. Then, in their next appearance, they came back and embarrassed Virginia 130–85 in what Loughery called "the perfect game."

A pattern was emerging both for the Nets and for the league—inconsistency. The league officials oscillated between excitement and depression. Their hopes were buoyed by new owners, by signed draft choices, by impressive performances of little-known rookies, by hints from NBC of interest in a national television contract. They were depressed by unkept promises from backers, players reneging in contracts, disappointing crowds. Tedd Munchak's daily call to the league office from his own headquarters in Atlanta was like a good-news, bad-news joke.

The Nets oscillated between precision and inefficiency. They would play tight defense one night and stand around watching a lesser team run by them the next. Julius admitted, "I don't have the overall quickness and strength night after night that I used to. I know I have bad knees, so I have to take some precautions." On too many nights it appeared that his healthier teammates were also taking precautions.

DeBusschere had privately expressed a lack of confidence in the style of Billy Paultz during training camp. He had acquired Otto Moore, an NBA reject, who he thought might provide the speed Paultz lacked. But Moore was cut before the season began. As the Nets were out-rebounded night after night, both in winning and losing causes, DeBusschere's discontent grew.

Loughery was also having trouble finding the right combination at guard. Brian Taylor seemed reluctant to shoot. Williamson provided muscle, but was unwilling to give up the ball to the good shooting front court. Melchionni was the best control guard, but sacrificed something on defense. Gale was spotty, Skinner was inexperienced.

Still the Nets were able to compile an impressive record and remain in a close race with the Colonels for first place. They won on the basis of individual talent and by taking advantage of the three weak teams in their division. But they were not gelling as a team. On most nights there was a lack of execution and camaraderie.

Over in the other league, the NBA, two former Nets were having the best seasons of their careers. Rick Barry was the only star left on a Golden State Warrior team that a year before was star-studded. Playing with rookies and unknowns, he was being hailed as playing the game better than anyone had ever played it. And he led his team to the best record in the west by all-star break time.

And Jim Chones, who had been a bust with the Nets and then with Carolina, had become the focus of a Cleveland team that two years earlier was the worst team in basketball and was now headed for the playoffs. Both Golden State and Cleveland were the two biggest surprises in all of basketball. And the two former Nets were largely responsible.

In late January, the Colonels came to Nassau, held Julius scoreless through the first eight minutes and took an early lead. Erving looked disoriented. But he began to convert from the outside in the second period and gave the Nets a lead by scoring 16 straight points in the third quarter. With just seconds left the game was tied, but Julius made two free throws to give his team a 112–110 win. He finished with 42 points, 18 rebounds, and 10 assists in what would be his best all around effort all season.

A week later, the Nets went to Denver and it was reported that Julius' knees were aching and he would miss his first game in two years with the Nets. But when the game started, he was out on the floor. Again he looked disoriented at the outset, and again he rallied his team in the third quarter, scoring 15 points. He finished with 22, and the Nets won 114–101.

Erving was still consistent, but no longer considerably spectacular. His ailments limited him. He saved his high-wire act for games against the challengers to the Nets' title and for crucial situations in games against the other teams. On the nights when his teammates needed him to, he was able to block his limited mobility out of his mind and control the game.

In a game in San Diego, the Nets found themselves involved in a defenseless, run-and-shoot contest. The score was tied after the teams had run back and forth for the allotted 48 minutes. It was still tied after the first overtime, and after the second, and after the third. To that point, Julius had played 61 of the 63 minutes and averaged a point a minute. But in the fourth overtime he was exhausted and could no longer function properly. He scored one more basket to finish with 63 points (his career high, and four short of a league record), but the Nets lost 176–166.

The Nets coasted through February and March, beating all the lesser teams, and splitting their games against Kentucky, Denver, and also Indiana. They continued to alternate holding first place with the Colonels. By the last week in March, however, they had managed to open up a five game lead.

On March 24, they lost to Denver at home, 114–111. Two nights later they lost to Kentucky by a point when Brian Taylor missed a shot at the buzzer. Two nights after that they lost in Memphis, 111–106. It was their first loss all season to any team in their division other than the Colonels. They lost again to the Colonels 126–95 for their fourth straight defeat. Julius had only 19 points in the game after averaging close to 35 against Kentucky all year. After that game he went to the hospital with a backache.

In less than two weeks, the Nets' comfortable five game lead over the Colonels dissolved. The two teams finished the season tied with 58 wins and 26 losses. The Nets' record was better than the previous season when they were divisional champions. But that record was deceiving. They had won 30 of 31 games from Memphis, St. Louis, and Virginia, and were only 28 and 25 against the other six teams.

Two nights after the regular season should have ended, the Nets traveled to Kentucky for a one game play-off for the division title. The game seemed meaningless and unnecessary. The Nets had lost the season series to Kentucky, six games to five, and so the Colonels would have the odd home game if and when they met in the semi-finals of the play-offs. So all this game would decide was who would each team face in the first round. The winner would face Memphis, the loser would face St. Louis. Neither team would be particularly worried about who they met. Kentucky did have some added incentive, having lost the title to the Nets a year ago. And their coach, Hubie Brown, was enjoying his first tenure as a head coach and had no intentions of being canned for losing as his predecessor Babe McCarthy had been.

Julius was out of the hospital and fit for the game. He scored 33 points. But Billy Paultz was injured and could play only 14 minutes, and Artis Gilmore took advantage of his substitute, Willie Sojourner. Gilmore scored 27 points, but more importantly, controlled the game by collecting 33 rebounds. The Colonels won 108–99. The Nets had lost every meaningful game down the stretch and were dethroned as divisional champions. But in pro basketball, the teams who qualify for the play-offs get a second chance. And the Nets still appeared to have the talent to succeed themselves. "We beat them four of the last five times we played them," said Brown, "but they're still the team we're most worried about."

St. Louis came to New York to begin the first round of the play-offs. The Spirits had not beaten the Nets in 11 regular season meetings. After the first play-off game, it was 12. But the Nets barely won (111–106), and the Spirits' three burly rookies (Barnes, Lucas, and Gus Gerard) gave the Net forwards a physical beating near the basket. Barnes, who was most disappointing against the Nets all season often scoring fewer than ten points, scored 41. It seemed like an off-night for the Nets. It would later seem as if it were an off-night for the Spirits.

In the next game, Barnes was dominant, and Julius played the worst game I had ever seen him play. He had scored just six points, when, with ten minutes left, Loughery decided to give up on him for the first time. Barnes had 37 points and 18 rebounds, and the Spirits beat the Nets 115–97 to even the series at one. The Nets were lethargic from the first jump ball. The frustration of the evening was perhaps best demonstrated by Wendell Ladner, the Net forward and court comedian, late in the fourth quarter. Wendell went diving after a loose ball and lost his sneaker. The Spirits recovered the ball and began dribbling toward their basket. Wendell picked up his sneaker, ran after them, and threw his sneaker at the ball. It knocked the ball away from a player and out of bounds. The ref called a technical. Wendell could not understand why.

The series switched to St. Louis, but the Spirits continued to out-rebound the Nets and again embarrassed them 100–89. One loss could have been a fluke. But this was getting out of hand. It got worse when the Spirits took a three-game-to-one lead, winning again 113–108. Julius had regained his poise and scored 30 and 35 in the two games, but it was Barnes who was dominating the series; and Freddie Lewis, who the Spirits would not have if they had acquired Melchionni, whose patient leadership kept his young team calm when the game got close.

The Nets came back home, one game away from elimination and utter embarrassment. In the first half of the fifth game, they outplayed the Spirits for the first time in the series. Still they could not mount a comfortable lead. There was a feeling in the arena, that if they could survive this game, they would destroy the opposition's newfound confidence and be able to rescue the series. But in the second half, the Spirits edged closer, and that feeling of optimism turned to dread. The Nets made innumerable foolish mistakes. It looked as if they would surely find some way to lose. And they did. In the last few seconds, with his team ahead by a point, and the opportunity to dribble the remaining time away, Julius traveled with the ball. The Spirits took the ball in bounds and worked for a final shot. It was passed to Lewis at the top of the key, 20 feet from the basket. He took a jump shot that swished through the net. The Nets lost 108–107.

This was the way this particular season had to end for the Nets, on a note of irony with Lewis burying them, and a note of surprise with the Spirits, whom they had beaten twelve consecutive times, beating them four consecutive times. "This was Ripley's believe it or not," DeBusschere said after the game in the dressing room. But that was overdoing it. Disaster had hung over the Nets all year. They always seemed to find a way to avoid it. Until now.

The players sat on the stools in front of their lockers in the dressing room after the game. Julius whispered to some reporters. Willie Sojourner cried.

"A lot of these dudes better get a good look at this place," said Red Thorn, the assistant coach, "cause this is the last time they are going to see it."

The Spirits then went on to lose to Kentucky in five games in the semi-finals while, in the west, Indiana was upsetting Denver in seven games. Kentucky only needed another five games before eliminating the Pacers to win their first title. They had gone through the play-offs losing only two games. Brown had saved his job. And it now looked as if the long-range dominance of the league that the Nets expected for themselves might be expected of Kentucky.

At the same time, Barry was leading the Warriors to a surprising five-game win over the Washington Bullets for the NBA title.

Julius went home for an off-season of rest and treatment once again. But the rest of the Net organization could not remain inactive this off-season. DeBusschere, whose role as general manager was never clearly defined, was drafted by the owners to succeed Munchak as the league's commissioner. Thorn accepted the head coaching job at St. Louis after Bob McKinnon resigned. It was a job Thorn had been offered the year before but turned down because he doubted the capabilities of the team. After they beat the Nets, he changed his mind.

So the job of restructuring the Nets was left to Boe and Loughery. A month after the season ended, they acquired Swen Nater, the center for the San Antonio Spurs and possibly the strongest man in the league. To do so, they were forced to give up Larry Kenon, the second most consistent player on the team, and Mike Gale. But rebounding had been the problem all year, and along with Gilmore, Nater was the league's most prolific rebounder. There was then an opening at forward opposite Julius. It appeared that Paultz was now expendable and would be traded for someone to fill that void. If a deal could not be made, Wendell Ladner would be exected to start—at least temporarily.

On the evening of June 24, 1975, an Eastern Airlines
727 jet out of New Orleans crashed in a storm before
reaching the runway at Kennedy Airport in New York.
Kevin Loughery was sitting in the living room of his
Huntington, Long Island, home watching live coverage
of the crash on television. He spotted a Nets' bag among
the collected luggage. He rushed to the phone and called
the Nets office to see if they had known anything. They
had. And Loughery's fears were confirmed. Wendell
Ladner had been visiting his parents in Necaise Cross-
ing, Mississippi. His father had taken him to New
Orleans and put him on that plane. Along with 111
other people, he was dead.

Julius and Billy Melchionni were pallbearers at his
funeral in Mississippi. A few days after that, the Nets
held a memorial service for him at a Long Island church
which was attended by team members and officials,
friends, and fans.

"Wendell was my protector on the court," Julius said
that day. "He wouldn't let anyone beat up on Julius
Erving. I was thankful he chose to play that role."

Wendell Ladner was an unpredictable blithe spirit.
People loved watching him perform in a basketball
game, although most of his best performances occurred
when the ball was not in play. The fans in Louisville
did not forgive John Y. Brown for trading him away.
Some team officials speculated that the deal had hurt
attendance, until the Colonels won the championship.

It was no different in New York. "He was the second
most popular player on our team," said Loughery, "even
though he was far from the second best. Everybody
loved to watch Wendell. I have two young sons myself,
and they always wanted to come and see him."

Basketball was Ladner's catharsis. He lost all control
of himself on the court. Playing forward opposite Julius,
he was the opposite extreme. Julius would control his
temperament no matter what the situation. Wendell

would look for situations to lose control of his. Off the
court he had a reputation for wild living. He was always
seen beside a beautiful girl or two. He was considerate
and amiable and it was impossible not to like him. Had
the Nets been able to trade for another forward, it is
likely that he would have been traded away before the
next season. And he would have certainly become a
crowd-favorite elsewhere. But none of that matters now.
It will not be the same without him around.

In the face of a tragedy like this, what happened to
the team last year is insignificant. Words that writers
use to describe losing in sports, words like disaster and
tragedy, seem inappropriate, over-dramatic, even inane.
The Nets losing in 1975 doesn't matter now. The only
loss that matters is Wendell.

14. Dr. J. Joins the NBA

The financial stakes in professional sports have become so awesome that all the other statistics that intrigued us as kids have become insignificant. None of us has ever tried to hit a Nolan Ryan fastball or run through the Steel Curtain defense, but we have all picked up a paycheck. We cannot measure ourselves against Pete Rose's 44 game hitting streak, but his $800,000-a-year salary fills us with a combination of envy and disgust.

It is an anathema of our times that the business of sports has come to overshadow the games. Occasionally we are blessed with a sporting event—Hank Aaron's pursuit of Babe Ruth's career home run record, the 1975 World Series between the Reds and the Red Sox, the string of Pittsburgh Steeler Super Bowl victories, the Borg-McEnroe rivalry in tennis—that is so irresistible it demands we temporarily turn our attention back to the arena. But in between these rare precious spectacles, the fiercest and most dramatic confrontations seem to take place in offices and boardrooms. The most potent weapons of our athletes no longer seem to be jump shots and home runs but words. Words, words, words. Contract negotiations, labor negotiations, players jumping teams, teams jumping towns, owners selling out, players selling out. The deal is the main event. And men become heroes or bums not by how they handle the ball but by how they handle their business.

It once seemed ironic that nothing Julius Erving accomplished on the basketball court attracted as much attention as the $3-million deal that brought him to the New York Nets in 1973. But what was once ironic has now become expected.

Through the 1975-76 ABA schedule, Julius Erving assembled the finest season of any forward—and possibly even any player—in the history of professional basketball. He led his league in scoring for the third straight year with a 29.31-points-per-game average. He finished among the top ten players in rebounding, field goal percentage, three-point field goal percentage, assists, steals, and blocked shots. But the most impressive talent in team sports is the ability of an athlete to lift his teammates above their individual potential. And in 1975-76, Erving led a mediocre Nets team past talented and balanced squads from Denver, Kentucky, and San Antonio and on to their second ABA championship.

Just a few weeks into that season, Net coach Kevin Loughery realized that trading for center Swen Nater was a strategic error. Nater's strength as a rebounder did not help this team so much as his lack of mobility hurt them. A unit that featured Erving and breakaway guards Brian Taylor and John Williamson needed to run, and Nater could not run. To obtain Nater, Loughery had sent a pair of quick players, forward Larry Kenon and guard Mike Gale, to the San Antonio Spurs. To assure Nater sufficient playing time, he later sent center Billy Paultz to San Antonio in exchange for forward Rich Jones, a burly, bruising forward who would make a major contribution to the Nets' success. But in retrospect, the total exchange was counterproductive. All it accomplished was to make the Spurs a well-balanced, high-scoring team with a great future.

Kentucky meanwhile, was coming off its first championship, and Artis Gilmore and his teammates had another training camp to perfect coach Hubie Brown's sophisticated patterns. And the Denver Nuggets, buoyed

by the transfer from absentee to local ownership and the
completion of the 19,000-seat McNichols Arena, had
added Dan Issel and prized rookies Marvin Webster
from Morgan State and David Thompson from North
Carolina State to a team that had already finished with
the best record in the ABA (65-19) in 1974-75.

Denver again won the most games during the regular
season. But the Nets, after defeating San Antonio in a
wild seven-game play-off semi-final that was marred by
fan violence in Texas, needed only five games to beat
the Nuggets for the title. That series was the high point
of Erving's career thus far. He won the first game with a
15-foot jump shot at the buzzer and put together five
games the likes of which no one had ever seen—45
points, 12 rebounds; 48 points, 14 rebounds; 31 points,
10 rebounds; 34 points, 15 rebounds; 31 points, 19 rebounds. All this while being guarded by the best defensive forward in either league, Bobby Jones, and while
effectively guarding David Thompson, holding the
leaper below his 27-point-per-game season scoring average. Erving won the Most Valuable Player award in the
play-offs for the second time in three years and the Most
Valuable Player award for the regular season for the
third consecutive year.

In another year at another time, Erving's dream season might have garnered the kind of national attention
received by Joe Namath when he lifted his teammates to
the 1970 Super Bowl title, or by O. J. Simpson when he
rushed for over 2000 yards, or by George Brett when he
flirted with a .400 batting average. But in the ABA in
1976, this was not to be. Like his accomplishments on
the Harlem playground and in the gym at the University
of Massachusetts and arenas in Virginia, the story of Dr.
J.'s greatest season would be limited to legend, spread
only by word-of-mouth by those who were fortunate
enough to have caught a glimpse of him. For 1975-76

was a season dominated by the business of basketball, the year the war ended, the year of the merger.

Observing Julius that season as general manager of the Nets, Dave DeBusschere, the former star of the Knicks, said, "If there is a merger, Julius will be responsible." It was a remark echoed throughout both leagues. And yet the man who instigated the basketball merger was also tainted by it.

"Our fans might be having a ball," Carl Scheer, the president of the Denver Nuggets, said at the beginning of the 1975-76 season. "But what they don't realize is, Rome's burning around us."

For while Julius Erving and David Thompson were thrilling the fans with their aerial shows, the American Basketball Association was hanging on by a thread.

The ABA had never been a league so much as a legal challenge. "From the outset," wrote Robert Carlson, the ABA's legal counsel and one-time commissioner, in the *New York Law Forum,* "the ABA . . . conceived and designed a strategy of conflict . . . to force a merger with the NBA." In many ways, this notion of merger was a carrot that owners looking to sell could wave in front of suckers looking to buy. The two professional basketball leagues had gone through the charade of preliminary merger talks soon after the ABA was established. But these talks were aborted in April of 1970 when the NBA Players' Association obtained a restraining order alleging the two leagues were "combining and conspiring to restrain trade in professional league basketball." The players proceeded to sue for damages, provoking a lengthy court battle that became known as the Oscar Robertson Case—named after the president of their association.

To some extent the NBA owners were content to hide behind this decision, hoping that the upstart ABA would eventually dissolve. Watching the ABA owners conduct business, this seemed like a safe bet. Very few of the men who bought into the ABA in the league's first few years seemed as concerned with operating a successful franchise as with profiting quickly from their investments. Don Regan, the law partner of the league's first president, Gary Davidson, bought an unlocated floating franchise for $6000, then sold it immediately to a group of investors from Louisville for $30,000 plus a 5 percent interest. Regan then sold that 5 percent to John Y. Brown, the owner of Colonel Sanders' Kentucky Fried Chicken, for an additional $35,000. There are few places where you can make a rapid 1100 percent return on your investment. Regan's profiteering was not unique— the ABA played host to a perpetual game of musical chairs for businessmen.

But men like Carl Scheer and Roy Boe of the Nets got into basketball planning to stay around for a while. Boe had convinced his partners to make the investment in Erving in 1973 in order to move his team out of the shadow of the NBA champion New York Knicks. And in just one year in Denver, Scheer had spun flax into gold, setting up an organization so skillful that owners of NBA teams sent their administrators there for training. Scheer said up front that his intent was to build such a strong franchise that the NBA would have to accept the Nuggets no matter what happened to the rest of the ABA. Boe obviously had the same tactic in mind. Both men had to be pleased to hear Sam Schulman, owner of the NBA's Seattle Super-Sonics, say, "The only things in the ABA any of us give a damn about are Denver and Julius Erving." But the two owners could only sustain themselves on talk for so long while no progress toward amalgamation was made. Finally, Boe and Scheer decided they had to take a rash step to protect their investments and investors. In September of 1975, they turned their backs on their colleagues and applied to the NBA as expansion franchises. "It was one of the blackest days in the history of our league," said one ABA administrator. The other ABA owners threatened lawsuits which eventually forced the turncoats to withdraw their applications. And although one of Scheer's partners said that this move started the process for an eventual merger, it also discouraged some of Scheer's and Boe's fellow ABA owners and left the survivors in a poor negotiating position. By midseason ABA franchises in Memphis and San Diego liquidated, and the Utah franchise consolidated with the St. Louis franchise. The ABA was reduced to an unmanageable seven teams and realigned into one division. It became apparent that this was the league's final season. In most of the towns where franchises remained, the fans lost interest in this dying business. (Attendance in New York dropped to 1500 a game during this championship season.)

While the ABA was crumbling, the NBA was in the process of solidifying itself. In early 1976 the NBA owners made an out-of-court settlement of the six-year-old Robertson Case, agreeing to pay their Players' Association $4.3 million, or about $250,000 per team. To some extent, this was the break that Boe and Scheer and their struggling colleagues needed. Basketball is still a cottage industry. It is played in indoor arenas where seating capacities often cannot produce enough income to meet a team's expenses. The average team grosses about $5 million a year, comparable to a large filling station. (National Football League teams get about that much from their network television contracts alone.) The budget of a professional basketball operation is so tight that in most cases profit can only come from playoff revenues—or expansion revenues. A sudden $250,000 debit can mean the difference between profit and loss. This unanticipated assessment for each NBA team had to come from somewhere—so why not take advantage of the desperation of the ABA owners? The irony here was that the players who had blocked the merger for six years were now forcing it.

And so in April of 1976, while the two leagues' play-offs were under way, the ABA negotiating committee of Scheer, DeBusschere—who was now the ABA commissioner—and Angelo Drossos—a stockbroker and president of the San Antonio Spurs—was invited to New York for a secret meeting with a committee of NBA owners. If the ABA representatives had any delusions about their value to the NBA, they were humiliated into sobriety by the opening remarks of Bill Alverson, the president of the Milwaukee Bucks. "I have no mandate from my colleagues to make a deal with you SOB's," Alverson said. "The NBA isn't a charitable organization, and if it's not good for the NBA then screw you! Don't give me that crap about it being good for the industry and the fans. It must be a good business deal or I'm not interested."

What Boe and Scheer had accomplished in New York and Denver was now virtually meaningless. The value of their own attractive franchises was nullified by all the fly-by-night ABA owners who, during the nine-year basketball war, had stolen players off NBA rosters and signed NBA draft choices and filed suits, meaningless and otherwise, in hopes of precipitating a quick merger. Alverson himself was still outraged by the settlement Boe made when he signed Erving in 1973—a deal in which compensation was paid to the Atlanta Hawks, who had signed Julius illegally, instead of to the Bucks, who had selected Erving in the NBA draft. "If they wanted to tell me Julius Erving and David Thompson were shit, I had to sit there and take it," Scheer said. "I was there with my hat in my hand and I knew it."

Throughout the next two months of play-offs, while Julius was putting on his greatest show against the Nuggets, there were half a dozen secret merger meetings and a hundred proposals made by one side and rejected by the other. The only party to make a constructive offer was the CBS television network, which hoped that Erving and Thompson would boost the sagging ratings of its NBA telecasts. CBS offered to up the ante on their four-year contract with the NBA from $43 million to $48 million if four "expansion" franchises were added.

This prescribed the first condition for consolidation: only four teams from the ABA (which was now down to six, with Julius' old team, Virginia, folding at the end of the season) would be admitted to the NBA. So the ABA owners were forced to negotiate all over the country at once. They had to lobby 17 NBA owners with diverse interests; they had to make an equitable settlement with John Y. Brown of Kentucky and Ozzie Silna of St. Louis, whose teams would be excluded from the merger; and they had to make the NBA demands of a $4-million entry fee and no television revenue for five years seem sensible to their partners and bankers.

The owners of the four teams under consideration—Boe of New York, Scheer of Denver, Drossos of San Antonio, and Bill Eason of the Indiana Pacers—were invited to the NBA owners' meetings at Hyannis, Massachusetts on June 13. At that point the only issue settled was the buy-out of John Y. Brown. Brown was in the process of a costly divorce from his wife, Elly, who he had once made the president of the Colonels in what turned out to be a publicity gimmick. Brown was outraged by the price of the consolidation, so he graciously accepted $3 million from the owners of the four surviving franchises.

The meetings at Hyannis were highlighted more by ego battles than by business negotiations. Many of the NBA owners seemed intent on getting psychic revenge on the ABA owners who had sent their player payrolls soaring over the past decade. The ABA owners proposed a dispersal draft of the 20 players under contract to Kentucky and St. Louis, with the proceeds going toward compensating the owners of those teams. The NBA owners balked at having to now pay money to acquire players they had drafted and lost to the ABA. When they left these unpleasant sessions with the NBA owners, the ABA representatives headed to fruitless meetings with Silna, who had shown up uninvited to protect his own interests. When the ABA owners returned to their hotel rooms, they spent the rest of their evenings on the phone with their partners and bankers, trying to sell them the possible deal.

Finally, the NBA asked an entry fee of $4.5 million over six years, which was reduced to $3.2 million in cash. The NBA agreed to a variation of the dispersal draft which demanded the first million as compensation for the teams that had lost valuable draft choices and the rest going to the dissolving ABA clubs. The numbers were outrageous, but the ABA owners had no choice but to accept them. Meanwhile Ozzie Silna was still holding out and thus improving his own position. Eventually Silna, who had paid $1.5 million for his franchise just two years earlier and ran a ragged operation that might not have survived another season, agreed to accept $2.3 million, plus one-seventh of the money the four ABA teams would receive from the NBA television contracts in perpetuity. This deal established Silna as one of the most financially successful owners in the history of pro basketball.

While this arrangement was being finalized, John Y. Brown showed up in New York and complained he was no longer satisfied with his settlement. Scheer flew to New York and spent all night in a shouting match with Brown. Brown agreed to settle for an additional $391,-000. Drossos refused to pay Brown another penny. Scheer, Boe, and Eason agreed to split this additional cost.

The manic desire to make the deal, to keep the teams in existence, had driven out all reason. With their terri-torial indemnity payment to the Knicks added to the other costs, Boe and his partners were obligated for $8 million, half of it to be payed before they ever played a game in the NBA. The dream of the original ABA owners to form a new league that could challenge and force a cheap merger with the NBA was just a bad joke now. Between the merger and the operating losses over the years, Boe would've been better off ignoring the ABA and waiting until he could acquire an NBA franchise for himself. It would've been cheaper. And it would've been a lot more pleasant.

The unpleasantness did not end for Boe with the merger. The excitement of having finally been admitted to the established league dissipated when Julius Erving did not show up for training camp. Julius and his agent, Irwin Weiner, contended that Boe had promised to renegotiate the star's contract from $350,000 a year up to $1.9 million for four years if the Nets were accepted into the ABA. Under the circumstances it seemed like poor timing on Erving's part. Given the burdens of the merger, Boe could not very well approach his partners with an additional expense. And the fact was that in Julius' three years with the Nets, despite two championships, the team had never drawn as many fans as they had seven years ago when Rick Barry played in the newly opened Nassau Coliseum.

Boe and his heavily mortgaged partners were outraged by Erving's demand. They refused even to talk to Julius, and tried to pressure him by negotiating through the newspapers. Julius had played his heart out for this team, and now felt he was being made out to be the bad guy. As is his style, he retreated from this distastefulness, hiding out in the new 17-room mansion he had moved his family to in Upper Brookville, on the Long Island Sound. But when the season was about to begin, Erving could hold out no longer. Against the advice of Weiner, he drove to the Nets' offices to confront Boe.

Boe refused to budge. Julius emerged announcing he felt "tarnished and used."

It was difficult to side with either man. Julius had heard all the talk about him being solely responsible for the merger. And in this era, there was no precedent of any other athlete being generous with his career. Boe, meanwhile was buried under a pile of financial obligations and had a legal contract with his star. And yet, if he entered the NBA without Julius on his team, the fans would stay away and the financial burden would get heavier.

Meanwhile, in Philadelphia, Pat Williams, the owl-faced general manager of the 76ers, saw an opportunity he could not pass up. Just three years before, Williams had lived through a nightmare season in which his team had won only nine games, a season in which he had been reduced to presenting a singing chicken and a dancing bear as a halftime show to try to attract an audience. But since that year, after which Kevin Loughery quit the Sixers to become coach of the Nets, Williams had been slowly rebuilding his franchise. He had drafted Doug Collins, a talented guard out of Illinois State in 1974, and signed George McGinnis after his contract with the Pacers expired in 1975. After four seasons without qualifying for the play-offs, the Sixers had won 46 games before being eliminated in the opening round of the play-offs in 1975-76. This season, the Sixers had added Caldwell Jones, a seven-foot center who had been tutored by his coach Wilt Chamberlain in San Diego and signed as a free agent when his ABA contract expired. And the team had just been purchased by F. Eugene Dixon, the heir to the $150-million fortune of the Widener family, builders of the Philadelphia trolley line. Williams knew he now had the resources to add the most exciting player in the sport to an already talented team. He went to Fitz Dixon to sell the idea. Dixon admitted he knew nothing about basketball. What he did know was horses. Williams compared Julius Erving to Man o' War. Dixon told Williams to go make a deal.

The 1976-77 season began. Erving refused to play for the Nets. Boe felt he had no choice but to trade his meal ticket. He offered Julius to the Knicks. Julius would have instantly revived that slumping franchise. But Mike Burke, the Knicks' president and a member of the NBA's merger committee, felt that taking Julius away from the Nets would destroy a franchise and hurt the entire league. Pat Williams was not so benevolent.

On October 21, 1976, Julius Erving signed a new $3.5-million six-year contract with the Philadelphia 76ers. Fitz Dixon paid Roy Boe another $3 million for the rights to the star, thus reducing the Nets' burden somewhat. Julius was immediately labeled "The Six Million Dollar Man" by the Philadelphia press.

"Would I be going too far to call this the most exciting, breathtaking team in the history of sports in our country?" Williams asked at the signing ceremony.

But while Williams gloated, Burke's fears for the Nets' future proved to be legitimate. Within three years, Boe's partners in Long Island Sports accused him of poor financial management and forced him to sell his interests in both the Nets and the Islanders of the National Hockey League. The Nets were eventually acquired by a group of investors from New Jersey that moved them from Long Island into the gym at Rutgers University, where they would stay until the new sports arena at the Meadowlands complex was completed in 1981.

When Boe sold Julius, my initial response was outrage. There are certain players who are so closely identified with a team that they should never be traded. The Dodgers should never have traded Jackie Robinson. The Giants should never have traded Willie Mays. The Braves should never have traded Henry Aaron. But with time I have come to feel compassion for Roy Boe, who built two good sports teams only to lose them before he could see the Nets succeed in the NBA and the Islanders win the Stanley Cup. He was a victim of the times.

Julius' departure made me wonder if it was worth being a fan at all anymore. I never was a fan of monikers and uniforms. It was players I rooted for. The players were the team. George McGinnis left his hometown, Indianapolis, because he could make more money in Philadelphia. Pete Rose left his hometown, Cincinnati, because he could make more money in Philadelphia. And now Julius was leaving his home because he could make more money in Philadelphia. It seems as if sooner or later they all end up in Philadelphia.

I had been able to rationalize it when Julius turned his back on his teammates in Virginia to come to Long Island. He was coming home. Home to his fans. Home where he belonged. As a kid growing up on Long Island I had dreamed of my favorite sport, pro basketball, being played in my home region, and he was going to make it happen. It seemed like the right thing for Julius to do back them. But now I had to wonder. In many ways, Julius' departure was the metaphor for what sports had become—he had had his greatest season, won a championship, and then taken his business elsewhere.

15. "Like Traveling with the Rolling Stones"

In past eras, the teams you loved to hate were those with an overabundance of talent. The Mantle-Maris Yankees. The Bill Russell Celtics. Every Montreal Canadians team. Any team that came up against these perennial champions was an underdog, and beating them was always sweeter than beating anyone else—for the players and for the fans. And yet, at the same time that we hated these superior teams, we had a certain amount of awe and respect for them. After all, the very best teams were assembled by the same process as the very worst—exhaustive scouting, wise drafting, patient nurturing, and shrewd trading.

But in the seventies, in the Age of Negotiation, a new method of building a successful professional sports franchise evolved. Through their associations, the players in all team sports negotiated away the restrictions that bound them to teams beyond the duration of their contracts. An open market was created. And the most valuable skill of sports management—an eye for young talent—went the way of the single wing and the red, white, and blue basketball. The free-spending owner could sit back and relax and let other teams develop young talent. And then, when the players matured and proved their worth, the man with money could buy the best.

Though we all relish the opportunities provided by an open market in our own jobs and our own buying habits, it somehow seemed inappropriate in sports. One of the more refreshing aspects of professional sports used to be that the richest men were not necessarily the most successful. The fact that Red Auerbach could sustain championship teams while the ownership of the Boston Celtics was unstable made his success all the more remarkable and noble. Even those of us who believe players deserve to make as much money as they can felt that sports lost some of its magic when money became more valuable than savvy. There could be no awe and respect for a team that was bought—only disdain.

The 1976-77 Philadelphia 76ers were the first blatant example of the sports spending spree. Fitz Dixon invested $10 million in the two best players in the history of the ABA—Julius Erving and George McGinnis. He spent another million to lure 18-year-old Darryl Dawkins directly out of Evans High School in Orlando, Florida. For the fans in Philadelphia, who just a few years before had to watch the worst team in basketball history, Dixon was right out of the old *Millionaire* television series—giving them unexpected riches. He appeared to have assembled a team that could not help but win a championship.

But playing on such a team is never as much fun as it might appear. For Julius Erving, shifting from the Nets to the Sixers required not just a change of uniform but a change in his perspective. While playing in out-of-the-way, out-of-the-spotlight settings, Julius was always somewhat of an underdog. The locale seemed to magnify his accomplishments. But now, with this Philadelphia team, greatness was expected of him.

"We were acknowledged to be—and acknowledged ourselves to be—the most talented team in basketball," Julius said. "And because of that we were going to be subjected to close scrutinization. The expectations were impossible to live up to. Losing was intolerable. And we never won by enough."

The other players felt ambivalent about accepting

Julius onto an already talented team. When questioned about the arrival of his friend from the ABA, McGinnis said, "Me and Julius will get along so well it will be un-believable." And in the next breath he said, "I never got my due in the ABA. It was always Julius' league."

To really subject the Sixers to close scrutinization was to see their limitations. Although they were overloaded with talent, most of the talent was in one area—scoring. With Erving and McGinnis at forward, Dawkins at cen-ter, and Doug Collins and high-jumping, ball-hogging Lloyd Free in the back court, the Sixers fielded the team of five players each of whom was ineffective and bored without the ball. The coach of this group, Gene Shue, was, of all the coaches in the league at this time, the least suited to meld these shooters into a unit. Shue had coached a frenetic, high-scoring Baltimore Bullet team that featured Earl Monroe, Gus Johnson, and Wes Un-seld, a team that relished offense, ignored defense, and never won a title. When Shue succeeded Kevin Loughery (who had played for him at Baltimore) as coach of the Sixers, he brought along his laissez-faire coaching philosophy. He sat back and watched his team play give-and-go basketball—Give me the ball and go to hell.

"The situation was created on day one in Philly that I would not play my game," Julius told Curry Kirkpatrick of *Sports Illustrated*. "I mean, here I was that very first week playing tough and going all out and playing my game when guard Fred Carter said to me, 'Hey, easy man. You're working too hard.' Then I found out what he meant. In Philly, when a man got hot and, you know, made three or four in a row, the defense didn't have to adjust to stop him because our offense made the adjust-ment to stop him—by not giving him that ball. When it was your time, you had to do it all, even if you were swarmed under with defenders. You did it then because you wouldn't see the ball for a long, long time."

Throughout Julius' first season with the Sixers, there

were riotous reports of the problems of trying to distribute one ball among all those shooters. In one game, against San Antonio, the Sixers had a wide lead when McGinnis failed to hit an open Collins on a fast break. As the team moved back to play defense, Collins yelled at McGinnis, "Pass the fucking ball, will ya!"

During the next time out, Collins complained and McGinnis was benched. McGinnis cursed at Collins as the team returned to the floor.

Surrounded by ego battles, Julius refused to assert himself. Ray Wilson had said that, as a child, Julius "never had to dominate a situation. He was never a threat to anybody." Now that personality was affecting his play. When Julius got the ball he was usually at the top of the key. Since his teammates refused to move without the ball, opposing defenses simply cut off the middle and blocked all lanes to the basket. His scoring average dropped from 29.31 in the ABA a year before to 21.6. One of the coaches who had seen him in the ABA joked that Julius' high-wire act had been given away as part of the merger agreement. His coach with the Nets, Kevin Loughery, wondered out loud, "What happened to the player I used to have?"

Julius' best performance all season was in the midseason All-Star game. There he put the ball to the floor, soared to the hoop, scored 30 points, and won the Most Valuable Player award.

As always, Julius was philosophical about his predicament. "What's right is if you're working for an organization, you have to take direction," he said. "You have to know when to employ your own judgment. What I wanted to do was what was best for the team and what the coaches wanted. My philosophy was to strive for consistency within the team concept and so I approached the game with less of a scorer's ego.

"Coming into the NBA broadened my perspective on people. Throughout this league there seemed to be guys with limited talent and exorbitant egos. We had much more solidarity in the ABA. We had a common bond—survival—so we didn't have time for egos. We were always being called second rate and trying to disprove that. When I saw the NBA ego, I said, 'I'm not going to be like that. Not ever.' I was just going to do what I was asked to do the best I could."

Despite the controversy and the dissension, the Sixers managed to win 50 games and their first divisional title since 1967-68. Preceded by stories of their follies in each town, they set a league record for road attendance that still stands, selling out 33 of their 41 road games. In the play-offs they beat Houston and Boston and met the Portland Trail Blazers in the finals. The series matched the two extremes of coaching styles: the selfish, one-on-one team of individual stars against the disciplined, precision team that played with more intelligence than finesse. The Trail Blazers were coached by Jack Ramsay, once the Sixers' general manager and coach, and one of the many men who had been influenced by the success of the Boston Celtic dynasty of the late sixties. Ramsay constructed his team around the passing talents of center Bill Walton, stressing constant movement without the ball on offense and full-court pressure on defense. As Erving had with the Nets, Walton inspired his teammates—who averaged just 23 years of age and 2 years of experience—to rise above their potential. Over the course of a season, the Trail Blazers had learned that by pooling their limited individual talents they could overcome less organized teams with more talent.

The Sixers won the first two games of the series in Philadelphia. Shue surprised the Trail Blazers by having his center, Caldwell Jones, dribble up the court, nullifying Portland's back-court pressure and drawing Walton away from the basket. The games were very physical, with Walton and Maurice Lucas wrestling with Dawkins, McGinnis, and Erving under the boards. The shoving came to a climax in the fourth quarter of the second game: Doug Collins and Portland forward Bob Gross went up together for a rebound and fell to the floor. The players jumped to their feet and squared off. Dawkins came to his teammate's aid. He threw a punch toward Gross that missed and hit Collins in the jaw. Then Maurice Lucas came up behind Dawkins, punched him in the back of the head, and sent him sprawling. When the series moved to Portland, the home team had control of the backboards. That punch seemed to have knocked the fight out of Dawkins. McGinnis was in an embarrassing shooting slump (16 for 48 in the first five games) which was worsened by needling from his teammates in practice. Suddenly, the Sixers all began looking for Julius. They gave him the ball and stood around waiting for him to do something. And although he averaged over 30 points per game for the series, it was not enough to overcome the Blazers' balance. Portland won the title in six games.

It is difficult to tinker with a team that in just one season together goes all the way to the sixth game of the NBA finals. So the Sixers began the 1977-78 season with the same personnel with which they finished the previous year. But throughout training camp and the first two weeks of the schedule (during which they won only two of six games), it was apparent that the ball distribution problem had not been solved. Few teams are willing to trade so early in a new season when they are still determining what their players can do. The only move available to Dixon was firing his coach, Gene Shue. He replaced Shue with 32-year-old Billy Cunningham. One of the most popular Sixers of all time, Cunningham had made the all-NBA team three times and played with Wilt Chamberlain on the 1966-67 team that had won more games than any team in history (68) and was voted the best basketball team of all time. Cunningham had retired prematurely in 1976 due to a knee injury. He was working as a commentator on CBS's telecasts of the NBA games, living in Philadelphia, and had remained friendly with many of the current Sixer players. When Julius and his family came to Philadelphia, Cunningham showed them around town and found them their Center City apartment. Cunningham is an affable fellow, and though he lacked coaching experience, Dixon and Williams hoped his personality was better suited to this gang of gaggling gunners than that of the aloof Gene Shue.

Most of the players were happy with the change.

"Warmth from the coach is important," said forward Steve Mix, a drinking buddy of Cunningham's. "It was getting stale with Gene here—we needed a change."

"We need a guy like Billy to put an arm around us and comfort us," said Doug Collins.

Only Lloyd Free, who after two years of politicking had finally convinced Shue to give him more playing time, seemed upset by the change. Cunningham called a team meeting as soon as he got the job. Free refused to show up, later claiming he hadn't known about the meeting.

For a few weeks, Cunningham had a honeymoon. The Sixers won four games in a row, lost to Washington, then won ten straight. Without the benefit of a training camp, Cunningham was stuck with Shue's style of play, with only minor variations possible. "Out of control basketball," Collins called it. Everyone attributed the streak to a new harmony. But when the team lost four straight in December, the bitching about lack of ball distribution and playing time started up again.

In one game, Cunningham grew annoyed watching Free—who had nicknamed himself "All-World"—hogging the ball. "Get under control, World," Cunningham yelled at him.

"I am under control," Free shouted back. Then Free ran by the bench and asked to be taken out. Cunningham jumped up and threw his hands in the air and said, "Who the hell do you think you are, Free?"

Cunningham's strategy was to keep everyone happy by giving the players on the bench more playing time. McGinnis quickly became disgruntled by the minutes he was asked to give up. He requested a closed-door meeting with the coach. He came out of the meeting and complained to the press.

There began to be rumblings that Cunningham's substitutions were predetermined and mechanical, that he lost control during the flow of a game. Practices were a circus, with Free putting on a dribbling show instead of running plays, McGinnis smoking and drinking Coke during shooting practice, Dawkins showing up in sweat pants held up by suspenders. But the fans kept coming, 15,718 a game, the highest average in Sixer history. On the road, the radios blared, the poker stakes went up, and fans and headlines greeted the team everywhere. One night in New Orleans, Jazz star Pete Maravich was benched with an injury, but a crowd of 35,000 still showed up at the Super Dome to see the Sixers. "This is like traveling with the Rolling Stones," said Chuck Daly, Cunningham's assistant.

They clowned and complained, they hogged and bickered. But despite themselves, the Sixers won 55 games and their second consecutive Eastern Division title.

"Any team that was looked at as closely as we were would've had problems," Julius said. "But because of our strength of character, we were able to win more games in two years than any other team. I think a lot of other teams given our circumstances would not have done so well. Things were written about us designed to cause problems. When people keep writing that your sixth and seventh men should be starters, they're going to start believing it.

"George [McGinnis] and I are friends and we talked about what was going on here a lot. We decided we would approach the game from a qualitative instead of a quantitative viewpoint. The guys who play the most minutes are always going to get the numbers. Truck Robinson plays 48 minutes a game and he wins the rebounding title. Pete Maravich plays 45 and he wins the scoring title. We knew that wasn't going to happen on this team. There's too much concern with minutes played in this league. What impresses me is the guy who ignores all that and plays his heart out when he plays."

Despite their fine overall record, the Sixers had slumped in the last two weeks of the season. Portland was hampered by a number of key injuries, including one that kept Walton out. Philadelphia had an opportunity to overtake them for the best record in the league, but lost four games in a row and six of their last eight. They seemed to have overcome their problems in the first round of the play-offs, beating the Knicks in four straight. In the Eastern Division finals, they met an aging Washington Bullet team that had learned to be aggressive defensively under new coach Dick Motta. In an interview before the series, Julius said, "Obviously you'd like to see me turned loose, have total freedom and be freaky. But what would be the result?"

Instead, Julius played meekly and was shadowed by forward Bobby Dandridge. Doug Collins had trouble scoring on Kevin Grevey, George McGinnis had another poor shooting series, and the Sixers bowed to the eventual champions in six games. After the sixth game, a reporter said to Julius, "Are you embarrassed?"

"Why should I be embarrassed?" Julius asked.

"Because you're a great team," the reporter said.

"I think that can be somewhat overstated," Julius said.

The fact was, these Sixers were not a great team. No one was able to play up to their ability. Julius had the most ability and he sacrificed the most. In his first two years in the NBA, he had 1507 fewer points, 663 fewer rebounds, 300 fewer assists, and 99 fewer steals than in his last two years in the ABA. His five-year ABA scoring average of 28.5 points per game was eight points above his NBA average.

"For me to sit in the stands and see his game go down the way it did hurt me," said his wife Turquoise. "It's like being married to an executive who's been demoted."

"I think what it might have been like if I stayed with the Nets," Julius told Curry Kirkpatrick of *Sports Illustrated* after that season. "I was the primary guy there. I think we could've been contenders for years because what we lacked in talent we made up for with Kevin Loughery's innovativeness. It was fun in the huddles when all else failed and Kevin would say to me, 'It's time for you to do something.' And you know, I would. But I refuse to be pressured into taking over here. I'm a follower."

There were the expected comments around the league that Julius had lost his talent, or that he had shone in the ABA only because it was a weak league. But none of these comments came from Cunningham. He was drained at the end of the season and refused to go through another year of chaos. He spent the off-season looking at films and deciding how to reshape his team to his own philosophies. He sought a much more disciplined approach than the Sixers had had under Shue. "To have a championship team, you have to handle every phase of this game," Cunningham said. "You cannot excel in one area and ignore others. You have to be consistent on offense and defense. Julius Erving is one of the most levelheaded players I have ever known. He understands himself and he understands his teammates. I can think of no one I'd rather build a team around."

"We were not building a good team here," Pat Williams finally admitted. "We had this bizarre carnival atmosphere. We had a great attraction but not a great team.

"When you have Julius, you have to shape around

him. He has a presence about him. A quiet dignity. He leads by hard work. In the past, Julius, McGinnis, and Free all wanted to be the main man. But you only have one main man on a basketball team, and we knew who it had to be."

During the off-season, the Sixers traded McGinnis and a number one draft choice to the Denver Nuggets for Bobby Jones, the best defensive forward in the league, and Ralph Simpson, once the best shooting guard in the ABA but now heavier and slower. Moving Free was more difficult. He had taken the brunt of the criticism for the Sixers' problems. But the day the season started, Williams found a taker—the one man who had always believed in Free, Gene Shue, the new coach of the San Diego Clippers. In exchange, the best that Williams could come up with was a 1984 first round draft choice.

"Let's face it," Cunningham said as he anticipated the new season. "This is now Julius Erving's basketball team. George sacrificed a lot of his game for this team. And Lloyd Free may win the scoring title in San Diego. But I did what was best for my team. The Nets were Julius Erving's basketball team—and all he did for them was win championships."

16. Doc's Team

In a game early in the 1978-79 season, the Philadelphia 76ers were trailing the San Antonio Spurs, the league's highest scoring team, by 11 points in the fourth quarter. During the previous two seasons, this would have been the time for confusion, the time when court sense turned to nonsense, the time when an overly talented basketball team turned into a three-ring circus. George McGinnis wanted the ball. Lloyd Free wanted the ball. Julius Erving wanted the ball. Whoever got it kept it.

Now only Erving remained, and he got the ball at the top of the key. His teammates all stood left of the lane as if they were lined up outside a movie theater. The entire right side of the court was left at Erving's disposal. Mark Olberding of San Antonio took a step back, daring Erving to shoot from 17 feet. Erving did, gracefully arching the jump shot that had improved with age through the net.

The next time down the floor, Erving received the ball near the right sideline. Again his teammates cleared out of the area to give the Doctor room to operate. This time Olberding set up nose-to-nose with Erving. One dribble, one quick step around the defender, and Erving went up into the air. Two Spurs went up with him, leaving two Sixers unguarded. Erving kept the ball at his hip, dropped it off to Henry Bibby, who then hit an open Doug Collins for a twelve-foot jump shot.

Following a Spurs' scoring spree, the Sixers went to

Erving at the top of the key again. This is where he can be most effective. When an offensive player gets the ball on the side of the floor, defenders on the opposite side leave their men and clog the middle in an illegal but effective zone defense that limits the paths the man with the ball can take to the basket. The man covering the player with the ball also has the sideline to use as a sixth defender. But at the top of the key the defender gets no help from either the sideline or sagging teammates. If the Spurs left their men, the ref could easily have detected a zone.

This time Erving used the available space to his right. He dribbled toward the basket, stopping and starting, then abruptly halted and pushed off his left foot into the air. Two Spurs went into the air with him. Erving slipped his left arm beneath their outstretched arms and flicked the ball underhand toward the rim. It bounced off the rim, but Darryl Dawkins—whose man had ignored him to help out on Erving—was hanging in the air alone, waiting to push the rebound through the steel hole.

Again and again, Erving received the first pass on the wing or at the top of the key. Even Collins, a talented clutch shooter sporting a 23-point-per-game scoring average, deferred to Erving in this critical situation. "He plays with the same cool look on his face in every situation," Collins said. "Me, I'm exciteable. I look to him down the stretch." Erving drove, pulling up for bank shots or dropping the ball off to teammates who kept in motion, knowing he would find them. In effect, the six-foot-six forward was now acting as his team's playmaker—all the 76ers were functioning off his moves.

With 39 seconds left, the Sixers had taken a 116-115 lead. But by now the Spurs had caught on to their opponents' ploy. Still another pass headed toward Erving. San Antonio guard Mike Gale got in the way of the pass and deflected toward his teammate George Gervin, who scurried down the floor like a scared rabbit. Gervin screeched to a halt and went up for a seemingly certain eight-foot jump shot. At the same instant, Erving left the floor at the foul line, soared toward Gervin, and swatted the shot into the crowd. Shaken by this unexpected blocked shot, the Spurs inbounded the ball and threw up a bad shot. Erving took the rebound and ran out the clock. The Sixers won.

Erving was chosen star of the game and interviewed on the postgame radio show that was boomed throughout the Spectrum, the Sixers' home arena. There had been only 11,000 fans in the 18,000-seat building that night. Although the Sixers were now off to a 5 and 1 start, attendance was already down 2,000 per game from the previous year. The interviewer asked Julius Erving why.

"We're not the awesome-looking team we were the last few years," Julius said in a concerned deep baritone. "We have to work much harder to win now. But we're not looking to be spectacular. We're looking to be consistent. In the past we had no direction at the end of close games. Now we do—I'm the primary target and Doug Collins is next. This direction makes us a better team. It's gonna be a lot more challenging and I'm ready to accept that challenge."

Julius paused, but before another question was asked, he addressed the fans directly: "We're gonna give you a good show every night, fans. Don't worry about that. So come out and see us."

I caught up with Julius the next day beside the pool at his Center City apartment. He sat in a blue velvet bathrobe, watching his three children—Cheo, Julius, Jr., and Jazmine—playing in the water. We had seen each other a few times over the years since he had resisted cooperating with me on the first edition of this book. He had always been cordial and eager to talk about the old days in the ABA. (In fact, I had always found the players who had played in that struggling league eager to talk about those days, as if they represented simpler times. The reminiscences were accompanied by the amused grins most of us wear when we recall high school.)

Julius seemed much more relaxed now that the 76ers had been reconstructed around his talents. He seemed grateful for the defensive help provided by Bobby Jones and for the slick ball-handling provided by Maurice Cheeks, a rookie guard out of West Texas State. His wife, Turquoise, had told me that he treasured his new role as team captain. "He never called me about any of the honors he won before," she said. "But when Billy told him he was captain, he called from practice to tell me."

"The situation I'm in now is very nice," Julius said. "There are very few players in better situations. I'm not trying to prove anything. I'm just trying to win. Proving doesn't enter into my thinking. I'm beyond that."

"You are not as spectacular as you once were," I said. "Can you still do the high-wire act you used to do?"

"I'd say I'm more calculating with the things I do now," he said. "Don't worry. I can still take off from the foul line and dunk, but I'm less prone to commit myself early. There are very few times when I take a rebound, dribble the length of the floor, and dunk like I used to with the Nets. That's not how I'm thinking now."

As we talked, it became apparent that during the bad times on the Sixers in the past two years, Erving had been studying the game and learning. While many of his teammates were going berserk, he was calmly acquiring new insights into his profession. "The game's changed dramatically in recent years," he said. "Guys are clogging the middle now, playing more zones. This game is about exploiting the weaknesses of the other team.

"When players get better, when they move from one level to the next, it's not because they run faster, jump higher, or shoot straighter. It's because they learn the game and apply what they've learned. I've learned when to look for daylight and when not to. All I want to be now is consistent."

"Don't you feel that you have something to prove now that McGinnis and Free are gone?" I asked.

"Maybe subconsciously," he said. "But I don't get caught up in it." He talked with his kids a moment, then turned back to me and asked, "So what do you think of our team now?"

"I think you're doing the things you have to do to win in this league," I said. "You're playing a swarming, rotating defense, you're spreading the scoring around and the replacements fit right into the starters' roles."

"Don't expect too much too soon," he said. "We're developing something here, but it's going to take time. It takes time to learn to play together. We have to be patient and so do the fans."

Erving's reserve proved to be wise. The Sixers led their division for the first few months of the season, getting off to a 24-11 start. But when Collins, the only consistent offensive performer besides Erving, was sidelined with a leg injury, the team collapsed and played only .500 ball the rest of the year. This team which was once overcrowded with offense, was now in need of offense. Without Collins' outside shooting as a threat, all those isolation plays to Erving became less effective. The consolidation of the two professional basketball leagues had improved the level of competition in the one resulting league. At the same time, an influx of smart, young coaches like Loughery and Hubie Brown of Atlanta and John McLeod of Phoenix, made the strategy of the game much more sophisticated, particularly on defense. In this league at this time, it was not possible for Erving to carry a team alone as he had once carried the Nets. With Collins lost, Julius had his worst season in 1978-79. Though his scoring average improved from 20.1 to 23.1, his overall play was less effective. For the first time in his career, Erving failed to be voted to an all-league team. The Sixers dropped to 47 and 35, the worst record since Julius arrived in Philadelphia, and they were eliminated by the Spurs in the Eastern Conference semi-finals.

But Julius was not shaken by the off year. He was convinced that this team was building intelligently for the future. And during the summer he had found new solace in his life. "I attended a family reunion and met more than 300 blood relatives," he told John Papanek of *Sports Illustrated.* "There were people I didn't even know who really cared about me and made me aware of my family history. Some of them shared their feelings about what was happening in my life and my career and why I was in the position I was in. I had asked myself many times, 'Who am I?' 'What does Dr. J. mean?' My Uncle Alfonso really simplified it for me. He said, 'Somebody along the line really laid a blessing on you. It was as if my great-grandmother or great-grandfather had said, 'Two generations from now the first son of the second son will be blessed.' That got me interested in the Bible again, and eventually I accepted Jesus into my life and all the mysteries became clear. I can sit in clear conscience with what I have knowing I am representing God. If it's happening to me, then it's happening to Him."

The Sixers made no major changes for the 1979-80 season. Cunningham and Williams both acknowledged, as Julius had, that it would take time to get comfortable with a new style of play. And they were a more cohesive unit that season. Cheeks matured into a capable ball-control guard and Darryl Dawkins, still only the age of most rookies, seemed to gain confidence. Collins never fully recovered from his injury, and at midseason the Sixers acquired guard Lionel Hollins from Portland to complement Julius on offense. Julius has his best offensive season in the NBA, averaging 26.9 points per game. Only Wilt Chamberlain had had a more productive season as a Sixer when he averaged 33.5 in 1965-66. The Sixers finished with 59 wins, the most in 14 years. But that was two games less than division rival Boston won.

Patiently, Red Auerbach had assembled another outstanding team in Boston. This season he had added rookie Larry Bird, the six-foot-nine college player of the year at Indiana State in 1975, and Rick Robey, a brawling six-foot-ten center-forward, who did not fit in with the Indiana Pacers. Combined with veterans Dave Cowens and Cedric Maxwell, this gave the Celtics the deepest and bulkiest front line in the league. Auerbach had also hired Bill Fitch, the clever former coach of the Cleveland Cavaliers, who designed a breakneck offense that capitalized on the big men's rebounding talents.

As anticipated, the Sixers and Celtics reached the Eastern Division finals. Quite unexpectedly, the Sixers handled the Celtics with ease, running over them in just five games.

In their second NBA final since Julius had arrived, the Sixers went up against the Los Angeles Lakers, a team buoyed by the arrival of six-foot-nine rookie guard Magic Johnson. Johnson, an effervescent 20-year-old who had led Michigan State to the NCAA title as a sophomore and then jumped to the pros, seemed to rekindle childish enthusiasm in Kareem Abdul-Jabbar and his teammates. With fine shooters like Jamaal Wilkes and Norm Nixon opening up the middle and Johnson making surprise passes, this was the best team that Jabbar had played on in his 12 years as a pro.

The Sixers and Lakers split the first four games of the series. In the fifth game, in Los Angeles, an intense, seesaw battle, Julius and Kareem had their best night of the series, scoring 36 and 40 points respectively. But in the fourth quarter of that game, Jabbar sprained his ankle. He would sit out the sixth game in Philly to try to get ready for a seventh in L.A. It was apparent to any basketball fan that this championship would be decided in the seventh and final game. After all, how could the Lakers compete with the Sixers without Jabbar? For the sixth game, rookie coach Paul Westhead pulled a surprise, moving Magic Johnson from guard to center. The Sixers, who had devoted so much time to designing a strategy to combat Kareem, looked disoriented from the opening minutes of the contest. They fell behind early and could never recover. Johnson scored 42 points and won the series' MVP award as the Lakers won 123-106.

Several things were apparent after this season: the Sixers had now made the transition from the offensive-minded team of the McGinnis-Free seasons to an all-around team that played the style of full-court ball required to win in the NBA, but they were missing scoring from the guard position and experience at center.

In the first round of the 1980 draft, the Sixers selected Andrew Toney, a six-foot-three shooting guard out of southwestern Louisiana who could give Erving the offensive support missing since Doug Collins first became injured. At center, they depended on Dawkins to continue to mature.

At the same time, the Celtics were adding still more depth to that burly front line. When Dave Cowens retired, Red Auerbach pulled off a steal of a trade, obtaining seven-foot center Robert Parish from Golden State. And in the first round of the draft he selected six-foot-eleven Kevin McHale, a strong rebounder and nagging defensive player, out of Minnesota.

Julius had what many people considered the outstanding season of his career in 1980-81. He had had more spectacular seasons in the ABA, and better years statistically, but he had now become a player with rare insight into the game, a player who could assume whatever role was demanded—scorer, play-maker, rebounder—on any given night. His fellow players confirmed his brilliance by voting him the most valuable player in the league. It was the first time in 17 years, since Oscar Robertson won the honor in 1964, that a player other than a center was voted MVP. The Basketball Writers of America also selected Julius for their all-time NBA team. He and Kareem Abdul-Jabbar were the only active players who joined centers Bill Russell, Wilt Chamberlain, and George Mikan, forwards Elgin Baylor, Bob Pettit, and John Havlicek, and guards Jerry West, Oscar Robertson, and Bob Cousy on the roster.

The Sixers and the Celtics each finished the season with 61 wins. Boston won the division title by beating the Sixers on the last day of the season, 98-94. The Sixers won a miniseries from Indiana in two games and a tough semi-final series from Milwaukee in seven games to qualify for the Eastern Conference finals against Boston. Philadelphia jumped off to a three-game-to-one lead in the series and it appeared as if they would embarrass the Celtics for the second year in a row. The Celtics were effectively defensing Erving, holding him to 12 points in the second game, but Toney's outside shooting and Dawkins inside play carried the team. And then the Sixers lived through a nightmare. They built good-sized leads early in each of the next three games, only to lose 111-109, 100-98, and 91-90. While Larry Bird was averaging 27 points per game, Cedric Maxwell was holding Julius below 20. The Celtics went on to defeat Houston in six games for the NBA title and the Sixers went home frustrated again.

Toward the end of the season, Fitz Dixon had awarded Julius with a new contract running through 1985 at a million dollars a year. The discomfort that plagued Erving and his family for their first few years in Philadelphia has subsided now and Julius is committed to the city and the team. He recently sold his house on Long Island and moved his family, which now includes four children, to Philly. He has set up an office there to run his outside businesses and opened Dr. J.'s Shoe Salon. One magazine recently estimated his personal worth at $10 million. In his spare time he is the national chairman of the Hemophilia Foundation, the coach of the Special Olympics basketball program, an adviser to the March of Dimes, a spokesman for the Lupus Foundation, the American Dental Association, the Philadelphia Police Athletic League, and an endorser of the American Red Cross, Population Institute, and Pennsylvania Adult Education. At 32, he seems to have found his way in his personal life, his personal business, and his game. He has erased the doubts of those who thought he had left his talent in the ABA and, through his community work and giving attitude toward all those he comes into contact with, erased the taint of having walked away from two teams for a higher salary.

The one thing still missing from his life is an NBA championship. He came within one point of it this year. But Dr. J. will not leave it at that. The legend is established, but the story still needs an ending.

Appendix

Julius Erving

College Basketball Record (University of Massachusetts)

Season	Games	Rebounds	Avg.	FG	FT	Pts.	Avg.
1969-70	25	522	20.0	238	167	643	25.7
1970-71	27	527	19.5	286	155	727	26.9

Professional Basketball Record
American Basketball Association

Season-Team	Games	Mins.	2 Pt. FG M-A	Pct.	3 Pt. FG M-A	Pct.	FTM-FTA	Pct.	Reb.	Ast.	Pts.	Avg.
71-72 Virginia	84	3,513	907-1,810	.50	3-16	.19	462-627	.75	1,319	335	2,290	27.3
72-73 Virginia	71	2,993	889-1,780	.50	5-24	.21	475-612	.78	867	298	2,268	31.9
73-74 New York	84	3,398	897-1,742	.52	17-43	.40	454-593	.77	899	434	2,299	27.4
74-75 New York	84	3,402	914-1,806	.51			486-608	.80	914	462	2,343	27.9
75-76 New York	84	3,244	948-1,873	.51			530-662	.80	925	423	2,462	29.3
National Basketball Association												
76-77 Phil.	82	2,940	685-1,373	.49			400-515	.77	695	306	1,770	21.6
77-78 Phil.	74	2,429	611-1,217	.50			306-362	.85	481	279	1,528	20.6
78-79 Phil.	78	2,802	715-1,455	.49			373-501	.75	564	357	1,803	23.1
79-80 Phil.	78	2,812	836-1,614	.52	4-20	.20	420-534	.79	576	355	2,100	26.9
80-81 Phil.	82	2,874	794-1,524	.52	4-18	.18	422-536	.79	657	364	2,014	24.6
81-82 Phil.	81	2,789	780-1,428	.55	3-11	.27	411-539	.76	557	319	1,974	24.4
82-83 Phil.	72	2,421	605-1,170	.52	2-7	.29	330-435	.76	491	263	1,542	21.4
83-84 Phil.	77	2,683	678-1,324	.51	7-21	.33	364-483	.75	532	309	1,727	22.4
84-85 Phil.	78	2,535	610-1,236	.50	3-14	.21	338-442	.77	414	233	1,561	20.0

Playoff Record

American Basketball Association

Season	Team	G	Min	FG	Pct	3FG	Pct	FT	Pct	Reb	Ast	Pts	Avg
71-72	Virginia	11	504	146-280	.52	1-4	.25	71-85	.84	224	72	366	33.3
72-73	Virginia	5	219	59-109	.54	0-3	.00	30-40	.75	45	16	148	29.6
73-74	Virginia	14	579	156-294	.53	5-11	.46	63-85	.74	135	67	390	27.9
74-75	New York	5	211	55-113	.49	0-8	.00	27-32	.84	49	17	136	27.4
75-76	New York	13	551	162-320	.50	4-14	.29	127-157	.81	164	69	451	34.6

National Basketball Association

Season	Team	G	Min	FG	Pct	3FG	Pct	FT	Pct	Reb	Ast	Pts	Avg
76-77	Phil.	19	758	204-390	.52			110-134	.82	122	85	518	27.3
77-78	Phil.	10	358	88-180	.49			42-56	.75	97	40	218	21.8
78-79	Phil.	9	372	89-172	.52			51-57	.76	70	53	229	25.4
79-80	Phil.	18	694	165-338	.49	2-9	.22	108-136	.79	136	79	440	24.4
80-81	Phil.	16	592	143-301	.48	0-1	.00	81-107	.76	114	54	367	22.9
81-82	Phil.	21	780	168-324	.52	1-6	.17	124-165	.75	156	99	461	22.0
82-83	Phil.	13	493	95-211	.45	0-1	.00	49-68	.72	99	44	239	18.4
83-84	Phil.	5	194	36-76	.47	0-1	.00	19-22	.86	32	25	91	18.2
84-85	Phil.	13	434	84-187	.45	0-1	.00	54-63	.86	73	48	222	17.1

Index